WILLIAMS
SONOMA

CALIFORNIA

EVERYDAY
SLOW COOKING

KIM LAIDLAW

PHOTOGRAPHY BY
JOHN KERNICK

weldon**owen**

CONTENTS

Quinoa Risotto with Chicken, Pesto, Asparagus & Lemon (page 79)

MODERN SLOW COOKING

Slow cookers are as popular today as when they were first introduced nearly fifty years ago. This hands-off cooking method promises easy preparation and delectable results and has long been the smart—and busy—cook's choice for transforming tough cuts of meat into tender, flavorful dishes. The slow cooker remains the go-to appliance when it comes to preparing consistently delicious and universally satisfying family meals. It is reponsible for the very best in everyday cooking and adapts particularly well to the modern techniques and dynamic range of fresh, seasonal ingredients favored by a new generation of adventurous home cooks.

The recipes in these pages offer delicious proof of this current evolution of slow cooking. Old-school beef tacos now feature Korean seasonings and spicy slaw, simple spareribs are lacquered with a tamarind glaze, and everyday beef round is slowly braised and then paired with a bright-tasting, colorful salad of arugula and blood oranges. A long-simmered *ragù* is still a slow-cooker favorite, but nowadays it's made with succulent pork shoulder instead of beef, and it's served atop greens rather than pasta. Stews have long been a hallmark of the slow cooker, but many of the ones you'll find here have a decidedly Asian profile, such as bowls of beef and udon fragrant with ginger, ramen and pork laced with garlic and green onions, spicy *pho* packed with braised chicken and cilantro, and a *bánh mì*–inspired blend of lemongrass-infused pork and pickled vegetables. Even desserts—gently spiced fruit butters, creamy cheesecake, silky custards—have a place in the contemporary slow cooker.

What these modern slow-cooker recipes share is a focus on the fresh flavors, ethnic influences, and seasonal ingredients that inspire today's cooks. That means that while they continue to yield results that are not unlike their fork-tender, easy-to-assemble counterparts of the early 1970s, they also feature an international pantry of seasonings, an enticing array of easy side dishes, and dozens of innovative garnishes. The outcome is a collection of new favorites that are every bit as convenient, economical, and wonderfully tender as those of the past but also reflect the fresh tastes, bright colors, and global flavors of the modern table.

MAKING MEMORABLE MEALS

The great thing about a slow cooker—and why I use mine often—is that you can add your ingredients and then leave the house while the food cooks. Through trial and error, I've found that a little additional prep goes a long way toward achieving superior results. This is not a "dump it all in and walk away" kind of book. While I've done my best to keep the recipes simple for today's busy lifestyle, I have also made sure that the dishes will become favorites of everyone at your table. A few extra minutes spent browning meat and vegetables on the stovetop before adding them to a slow cooker, for example, results in a rich brown crust on meat and can build the foundation for a sauce that will add a ton of flavor to the finished dish. Here are some more tips that will help ensure standout meals.

Prep all of the ingredients in the recipe before you start cooking. You might even prep them the night before to make putting the dish together in the morning even easier (just keep them covered in the fridge overnight). Cut vegetables like carrots, potatoes, cauliflower, or butternut squash into equal-size chunks—usually around 1 inch (2.5 cm) or so—to ensure even cooking.

Brown meat like chuck roast or pork shoulder in oil or butter before adding it to a slow cooker. This builds flavor by caramelizing the exterior of the meat and adds rich color to the finished dish. The same goes for sautéing vegetables like onions until golden brown, toasting spices until fragrant, or starting sauces in a frying pan (or the stove top–safe insert of a slow cooker), all of which help transform the ingredients and jump-start the cooking process.

Deglaze your stove-top pan with broth, wine, beer, vinegar, or another liquid flavor enhancer after browning the meat to release any caramelized meat juices or browned bits stuck to the pan bottom. This simple step helps maximize the flavor of a dish.

Walk away once you've covered the slow cooker, as recipes typically don't need additional tending. In fact, most recipes come out better if you leave the lid undisturbed during cooking so the heat stays consistent. Occasionally a recipe will call for one or two brief stirs during cooking, if possible, to ensure even doneness.

Skim the fat, shred the meat, and reduce the sauce. Taking a few minutes to finish a dish can make a big difference in both its taste and its appearance. Skim off as much fat as possible from the top of the cooking liquid using a large metal spoon. If you will be shredding or chopping the meat or poultry, transfer it to a cutting board and remove any bones, skin, gristle, or large bits of fat before you shred or chop. To perfect the sauce, strain the cooking liquid through a fine-mesh sieve, let stand for a few minutes to allow any fat to rise to the surface, and then skim off the fat. Simmer the strained liquid in a pan on the stove top until it thickens slightly, then spoon it over the finished dish.

STORING MEALS

I love the fact that a single slow cooker recipe usually makes enough for a full family meal and still leaves ample remaining for leftovers. Braised meats and poultry, soups, stews, and chilis will keep well in the freezer. Plan to serve beans, grains, vegetables, seafood, and desserts the day they are made, or store them in the refrigerator for serving again later in the week (usually within 3 to 5 days).

To store food in the freezer, let the food cool to room temperature, then transfer to an airtight, freezer-safe container. Make sure to label the meal, including the date it was prepared, and then store in the freezer for up to 3 months.

Lasagna with Beef Ragù, Kabocha
Squash & Crème Fraîche (page 38)

Bell Peppers Stuffed with
Quinoa, Black Beans
& Corn (page 127)

GETTING THE MOST OUT OF YOUR SLOW COOKER

Slow cookers come in various shapes and sizes. The recipes in this book were designed for and tested in an oval 6-qt (6-l) slow cooker with dual temperature settings, a ceramic cooking insert, and a tempered glass lid. The lid makes it easy to check on food without lifting it and releasing the built-up heat. Any browning steps were done in a frying or other pan on the stove top. Most of the recipes in this book yield six to eight servings, which means you can make dinner for tonight and, depending on your family size, have enough left over for another full meal (see page 8 for storage tips). Before using your slow cooker, read through its instruction booklet carefully. It will detail the product's features, information that will help you get the most out of the appliance.

Stove Top-Safe Inserts

Some slow cooker models feature a cast-aluminum insert that can be used on gas and electric stove tops. If you have one of these, you can do the initial browning in the insert, rather than in a frying pan as called for in the recipes. In most cases, you will need to brown the item in batches to avoid crowding. Be sure to check the manufacturer's directions before using your insert on the stove top. Most ceramic inserts cannot be used on the stove top.

Small Slow Cookers

In general, the recipes in this book will also work well in a 5-qt (4.7-l) or a 7-qt (6.6-l) slow cooker. If you are using a smaller slow cooker—3½ to 4 qt (3.3 to 3.8 l)—you will need to cut the recipe by one-third or one-half. Never fill the insert more than three-fourths full. The cooking time will remain the same.

Heat Settings

When making any recipe, follow the directions for temperature setting and for timing, as they are the keys to safe and successful slow cooking. Some recipes offer both a low-heat option and a high-heat option to make it easier to fit them into your schedule. The high setting is practical when you would like to speed up the slow-cooking process—often to about half the time of the low setting. I prefer to cook most recipes on the low setting, however, as it delivers fuller flavors and renders tough

cuts of meat more tender, plus today's slow cookers tend to cook at higher temperatures than older slow cookers. The high setting can cause the liquid to simmer rapidly, rather than slowly, and can lead to tougher protein, too much condensation, and disappointing results. If you do want to convert the low setting to the high setting, cut the time in half, check the results, then continue to cook for another hour if needed.

Different brands of slow cooker cook at slightly different temperatures, so you may need to adjust recipes accordingly once you get to know your slow cooker. If you are preparing the recipes in this book using an older model, you may find you must add to the overall cooking time, as it will likely cook at a slightly lower temperature.

Many models also have a warm setting that holds food at the ideal serving temperature, automatically switching to it when the cooking is done. Be sure never to cook at this setting.

ADAPTING RECIPES FOR A SLOW COOKER

The beauty of a slow cooker is that you can throw everything into it, set the timer, and leave the house, unlike conventional recipes that require tending as they cook on the stove top or in the oven. But your favorite stews, soups, and braised meats can be successfully adapted to a slow cooker by following a few simple steps.

- Choose a recipe that is slowly simmered, braised, or roasted.
- Tougher or fattier cuts, such as chuck roast, short ribs, brisket, pork shoulder, lamb shoulder, lamb shanks, leg of lamb, or dark-meat poultry, work best in a slow cooker.
- Select a recipe that is appropriate for the size of your slow cooker. For example, a recipe for chili that serves four can be doubled for a 6-qt (5.7-l) slow cooker.
- Reduce the amount of liquid by about half, as there is less evaporation when using a slow cooker. If the recipe doesn't call for liquid, add at least ½ cup (120 ml) broth or other liquid.
- If you have too much thin liquid at the end of cooking, pour it into a saucepan and simmer over medium-high heat until reduced and slightly thickened.

BEEF

HERBED MEATBALLS WITH TOMATO RAGÙ

Here you have two recipes in one, a tomato sauce infused with basil and oregano and succulent meatballs made even more tender with a long stint in a slow cooker. Give this recipe a modern twist by serving the meatballs and sauce over sautéed greens, or go old-school and serve them atop a pile of spaghetti.

FOR THE MEATBALLS

2 lb (900 g) mixed ground beef, pork, and veal

1 egg

1 small yellow onion, finely chopped

½ cup (1 oz/30 g) fresh bread crumbs or panko

¼ cup (1 oz/30 g) grated Parmesan or Romano cheese

2 tablespoons chopped fresh flat-leaf parsley

1 tablespoon chopped fresh oregano

1 tablespoon chopped fresh basil

Salt and freshly ground pepper

FOR THE RAGÙ

2 cans (28 oz/800 g each) crushed tomatoes with juices

1 can (15 oz/425 g) tomato sauce

3 cloves garlic, minced

1 teaspoon fresh oregano

1 sprig fresh basil

3 tablespoons small fresh basil leaves

SERVES 6–8

Preheat an oven to 450°F (230°C). To make the meatballs, in a large bowl, combine the ground meats, egg, onion, bread crumbs, cheese, parsley, oregano, basil, ¾ teaspoon salt, and ½ teaspoon pepper. Using your hands, gently but thoroughly blend the ingredients. Form the mixture into meatballs about 2 inches (5 cm) in diameter, placing them well apart on an ungreased rimmed baking sheet. (You should have about 24 meatballs.) Bake the meatballs until browned, about 10 minutes.

Meanwhile, in a slow cooker, combine the crushed tomatoes, tomato sauce, garlic, oregano, and basil sprig, and stir until combined.

When the meatballs are ready, transfer them to the slow cooker. Cover and cook on the low setting for 3 hours. The meatballs should be tender and cooked through in the center and the sauce should be slightly thickened. Remove the basil sprig.

Divide the meatballs and sauce among individual shallow bowls, garnish with the basil leaves, and serve.

MEDITERRANEAN OSSO BUCO

Osso buco, braised bone-in, cross-cut veal shanks, becomes fork-tender in a slow cooker. A specialty of northern Italy, it is classically finished with *gremolata* (parsley, garlic, and lemon zest) and served with saffron risotto. In this version, tart-sweet pomegranate seeds and fresh mint add bold flavor and crunchy texture to a warm orzo salad.

3 lb (1.4 kg) veal shanks, cut crosswise into pieces about 1½ inches (4 cm) wide

Kosher salt and freshly ground pepper

2 tablespoons olive oil

1 yellow onion, finely chopped

1 large carrot, peeled and finely chopped

2 celery stalks, finely chopped

4 cloves garlic, finely chopped

3 bay leaves

½ cup (120 ml) dry white wine

½ cup (120 ml) chicken stock

1 can (15 oz/425 g) diced tomatoes, drained

FOR THE ORZO SALAD

1 lb (450 g) orzo

1 teaspoon Dijon mustard

1 small shallot, minced

3 tablespoons red wine vinegar

Kosher salt and freshly ground pepper

¼ cup (60 ml) extra-virgin olive oil

1½ tablespoons finely chopped fresh mint

Seeds of 1 pomegranate (optional)

SERVES 6

Season the veal shanks generously all over with salt and pepper. In a large, heavy frying pan over medium-high heat, warm the oil. Working in batches if needed to avoid crowding, add the shanks and sear, turning once, until golden brown on both sides, 8–10 minutes. Using tongs, transfer the shanks to a plate.

Pour off most of the fat in the pan and return the pan to medium-high heat. Add the onion, carrot, and celery and cook, stirring often, until lightly golden, about 6 minutes. Add the garlic and bay leaves and cook, stirring, for about 1 minute longer. Pour in the wine and stock and stir to dislodge any browned bits from the pan bottom.

Transfer the contents of the pan to a slow cooker and stir in the tomatoes. Place the veal shanks and any accumulated juices on top. Cover and cook on the low setting for 6 hours. The veal should be very tender.

Transfer the veal to a plate and keep warm. Remove and discard the bay leaves, then transfer the contents of the slow cooker to a saucepan. Let stand for a few minutes, then use a large spoon to skim the fat from the surface. Place over medium-high heat, bring to a rapid simmer, and cook until slightly reduced and thickened, about 5 minutes.

Meanwhile, bring a large pot three-fourths full of salted water to a boil, add the orzo, stir well, and cook until al dente, according to package directions.

While the orzo cooks, in a small bowl, whisk together the mustard, shallot, vinegar, ¼ teaspoon salt, and a few grinds of pepper, then whisk in the oil to make a vinaigrette. You should have about ½ cup (120 ml).

Drain the orzo and transfer to a large bowl. Stir in the mint, two-thirds of the pomegranate seeds (if using), and enough vinaigrette to coat the orzo lightly.

Divide the orzo among individual plates and arrange the veal shanks on top. Garnish with the remaining pomegranate seeds, top with some of the cooking liquid, and serve. Pass the remaining vinaigrette at the table.

For a heartier presentation, omit the orzo salad and serve the osso buco over Creamy Polenta (page 173).

BRAISED BEEF WITH ENDIVE & SUN-DRIED TOMATO SALAD

In this dish perfect for a winter evening, pleasantly bitter endive, sun-dried tomatoes, and briny olives bring freshness, flavor, and texture to slow-braised beef bottom round. Serve it with spiralized Zucchini Noodles or Roasted Root Vegetables (both on page 174), or classic Mashed Potatoes (page 173) for a filling supper.

3 lb (1.4 kg) beef bottom round, trimmed of excess fat and cut into large chunks

Kosher salt and freshly ground pepper

2 tablespoons olive oil

6 cloves garlic, smashed

1⅓ cups (325 ml) beef stock

¼ cup (60 ml) dry white wine

3 fresh thyme sprigs

3 bay leaves

FOR THE SALAD

3 tablespoons olive oil

2 tablespoons walnut oil

2 tablespoons sherry vinegar

2 teaspoons Dijon mustard

Kosher salt and freshly ground pepper

2 large heads Belgian endive, cored and coarsely chopped

½ cup (70 g) green olives, pitted and chopped

½ cup (50 g) drained oil-packed sun-dried tomatoes, sliced

Grated zest of 1 lemon

2 tablespoons chopped fresh flat-leaf parsley

SERVES 6

Season the beef generously all over with salt and pepper. In a large, heavy frying pan over medium-high heat, warm the oil. Working in batches if needed to avoid crowding, add the beef and sear, turning as needed, until browned on two sides, 8–10 minutes. Using a slotted spoon, transfer the beef to a slow cooker.

Pour off most of the fat in the pan and return the pan to medium-high heat. Add the garlic and cook, stirring, for about 1 minute. Pour in the stock and wine and stir to dislodge any browned bits from the pan bottom.

Add the thyme sprigs and bay leaves and transfer the contents of the pan to the slow cooker. Cover and cook on the low setting for 6 hours. The beef should be very tender.

Just before the beef is ready, make the salad. In a bowl, whisk together the olive and walnut oils, vinegar, mustard, ¼ teaspoon salt, and a few grinds of pepper. Add the endive, olives, sun-dried tomatoes, lemon zest, and parsley and toss to mix.

Using the slotted spoon, transfer the beef to a cutting board. Let the cooking liquid stand for a couple of minutes, then use a large spoon to skim the fat from the surface. Using 2 forks, pull the beef into shreds, then transfer the beef to individual plates or a platter. Moisten the beef with some of the cooking liquid. Mound the salad on top of or alongside the beef and serve.

BRAISED BEEF WITH ARUGULA & BLOOD ORANGE SALAD

Here, tender shredded beef bottom round is paired with a flavorful salad of peppery arugula, sweet-tart blood oranges, hazelnuts, and avocado. You can substitute brisket or chuck roast for the bottom round with equally delicious results. Serve it alongside mashed sweet potatoes (page 173) for a more substantial meal.

3 lb (1.4 kg) beef bottom round, trimmed of excess fat and cut into large chunks

Kosher salt and freshly ground pepper

2 tablespoons olive oil

1 yellow onion, sliced

1 celery stalk, sliced

½ cup (120 ml) apple juice, preferably unfiltered

3 bay leaves

FOR THE SALAD

1½ tablespoons white wine vinegar

1 teaspoon honey mustard

Kosher salt and freshly ground pepper

¼ cup (60 ml) extra-virgin olive oil

4 cups (140 g) baby arugula

2 avocados, halved, pitted, peeled, and sliced

2 blood oranges, peeled and sliced crosswise into wheels

⅔ cup (95 g) hazelnuts, toasted and skinned, then coarsely chopped

SERVES 6

Season the beef generously all over with salt and pepper. In a large, heavy frying pan over medium-high heat, warm the oil. Working in batches if needed to avoid crowding, add the beef and sear, turning as needed, until browned on two sides, 8–10 minutes. Using a slotted spoon, transfer the beef to a slow cooker.

Pour off most of the fat in the pan and return the pan to medium-high heat. Add the onion and celery and cook, stirring often, until golden, about 6 minutes. Pour in the apple juice and stir to dislodge any browned bits from the pan bottom, then remove from the heat.

Add the bay leaves and transfer the contents of the pan to the slow cooker. Cover and cook on the low setting for 6 hours. The beef should be very tender.

Just before the beef is ready, make the salad. In a bowl, whisk together the vinegar, mustard, ¼ teaspoon salt, and a few grinds of pepper. Whisk in the oil. Add the arugula, avocados, oranges, and hazelnuts and toss gently to mix.

Using the slotted spoon, transfer the beef to a cutting board. Let the cooking liquid stand for a few minutes, then use a large spoon to skim the fat from the surface. Using 2 forks, pull the beef into shreds, then transfer the beef to individual plates or a platter. Moisten the beef with some of the cooking liquid. Mound the salad on top of or alongside the beef and serve.

BRAISED BRISKET WITH CHIMICHURRI

Brisket is a natural partner for the slow cooker, as a gentle braise renders it meltingly tender. Brightly flavored chimichurri sauce—a heady mix of herbs and garlic—and a scattering of cherry tomatoes provide the perfect fresh accent to the finished dish. If you like, stir a little lemon zest into the chimichurri.

1 point-cut beef brisket, about 2 lb (1 kg), trimmed of excess fat

Kosher salt and freshly ground pepper

2 tablespoons olive oil

1 large yellow onion, coarsely chopped

1 carrot, peeled and coarsely chopped

5 cloves garlic, smashed

1 teaspoon dried oregano

½ cup (120 ml) dry red wine

½ cup (120 ml) chicken or beef stock

FOR THE CHIMICHURRI

1½ cups (45 g) firmly packed flat-leaf parsley leaves and cut-up stems

2 tablespoons fresh oregano leaves

6 cloves garlic, quartered

¾ cup (180 ml) extra-virgin olive oil

Kosher salt and freshly ground black pepper

¼ teaspoon red pepper flakes

3 tablespoons white wine vinegar

2 cups (340 g) cherry or grape tomatoes, halved, for serving

SERVES 6

Season the brisket generously all over with salt and pepper. In a large, heavy frying pan over medium-high heat, warm the oil. Add the brisket and sear, turning once, until browned on both sides, about 10 minutes. Transfer the brisket to a plate.

Pour off most of the fat in the pan and return the pan to medium-high heat. Add the onion and carrot and cook, stirring often, until softened and lightly colored, about 6 minutes. Add the garlic and oregano and cook, stirring, for about 1 minute longer. Pour in the wine and stir to dislodge any browned bits from the pan bottom. Stir in 1 teaspoon salt, several grinds of pepper, and the stock.

Transfer the contents of the pan to a slow cooker and place the brisket and any accumulated juices on top. Cover and cook on the low setting for 9 hours, turning the brisket once halfway during cooking if possible. The brisket should be very tender.

Up to 4 hours before the brisket is ready, make the chimichurri sauce. In a food processor, combine the parsley, oregano, and garlic and pulse until finely chopped. (Alternatively, finely chop by hand.) Transfer to a small bowl and stir in the oil, 1 teaspoon salt, 1 teaspoon black pepper, and the red pepper flakes, mixing well. If serving right away, stir in the vinegar. If making in advance, cover and refrigerate for up to 4 hours, then stir in the vinegar just before serving.

Transfer the brisket to a cutting board and let rest for 5 minutes. Let the cooking liquid stand for a few minutes, then use a large spoon to skim the fat from the surface.

Cut the brisket against the grain into thick slices. Arrange the slices on a platter or individual plates and spoon some of the cooking liquid around the slices. Drizzle the slices with the chimichurri, sprinkle with the tomatoes, and serve.

KOREAN-STYLE SHORT RIB TACOS WITH NAPA SLAW

Rich, savory, and with a touch of spicy sweetness, these tender short ribs are braised with flavors found in Korean *kalbi*, thinly cut and marinated grilled short ribs. *Gochujang* is a fermented red chile paste that adds both heat and distinctive flavor.

5 lb (2.3 kg) English-cut beef short ribs

Kosher salt and freshly ground pepper

1 yellow onion, chopped

4 cloves garlic, chopped

1-inch (2.5-cm) piece fresh ginger, peeled and shredded

⅔ cup (160 ml) reduced-sodium soy sauce

⅓ cup (80 ml) mirin

3 tablespoons firmly packed dark brown sugar

2 tablespoons *gochujang*

1 tablespoon toasted sesame oil

FOR THE SLAW

1 small head napa cabbage

2 tablespoons rice vinegar

1 tablespoon *gochujang*

1 tablespoon canola oil

1 tablespoon fish sauce

1 teaspoon toasted sesame oil

1 teaspoon granulated sugar

Kosher salt

4 green onions, thinly sliced

¼ cup (15 g) chopped fresh cilantro

About 20 corn tortillas, warmed

MAKES ABOUT 20 TACOS; SERVES 8–10

Season the short ribs generously all over with salt and pepper. Put them in a slow cooker.

In a blender, combine the onion, garlic, ginger, soy sauce, mirin, brown sugar, gochujang, and sesame oil and process until smooth. Pour over the ribs and, using tongs, turn the ribs to coat evenly with the sauce.

Cover and cook on the low setting for 6 hours, turning the ribs once during cooking if possible. The beef should be very tender.

At least 45 minutes before the ribs are ready, make the slaw. Cut the cabbage lengthwise in half, cut out the core, and thinly slice crosswise. Put the cabbage in a large serving bowl. In a small bowl, whisk together the vinegar, *gochujang*, canola oil, fish sauce, sesame oil, granulated sugar, and ¼ teaspoon salt. Pour over the cabbage, add the green onions and cilantro, and toss to mix well. Set aside at room temperature for at least 30 minutes or up to 1 hour before serving. (The slaw can be made up to 1 day ahead, covered, and refrigerated.)

Transfer the ribs to a cutting board. When the ribs are cool enough to handle, remove and discard the bones, then, using 2 forks, shred the meat into bite-size pieces, discarding any large bits of fat. Transfer the meat to a bowl. Using a large spoon, skim the fat from the surface of the cooking liquid. Moisten the shredded meat with some of the warm cooking liquid.

To assemble the tacos, pile the meat onto the warmed tortillas, top with the slaw, and serve.

Offer small bowls of toasted sesame seeds, chopped fresh cilantro, pickled red onions (page 174), and *gochujang* to add to the tacos at the table.

CHIPOTLE CHILI WITH CORN SALSA

Canned chipotle chiles (smoke-dried jalapeños) in spicy adobo sauce impart a smoky-sweet flavor to this robust chili. Look for them in the Latin section of your favorite market. Any leftover chiles can be packed into an airtight container and frozen until the next time you have a craving for chili.

4 lb (1.8 kg) boneless beef chuck, trimmed of excess fat and cut into ¾-inch (2-cm) cubes

Kosher salt and freshly ground pepper

¼ cup (60 ml) canola oil

2 yellow onions, finely chopped

8 cloves garlic, sliced

2 chipotle chiles in adobo sauce, finely chopped

2 tablespoons chipotle chile powder

2 teaspoons ground cumin

1 teaspoon dried oregano, preferably Mexican

½–1 teaspoon red pepper flakes

1 cup (225 g) tomato paste

2–3 cups (475–700 ml) beef stock

Corn Salsa, for serving (page 175)

SERVES 8

Season the beef generously all over with salt and pepper. In a large, heavy frying pan over medium-high heat, warm the oil. Add half of the beef and sear, turning as needed, until browned on two sides, 8–10 minutes. Using a slotted spoon, transfer the beef to a plate. Repeat with the remaining beef and add to the plate.

Pour off most of the fat in the pan and return the pan to medium heat. Add the onions and cook, stirring often, until softened, about 6 minutes. Add the garlic and cook, stirring, for about 1 minute longer. Add the chipotle chiles, chipotle chile powder, cumin, oregano, red pepper flakes to taste, and tomato paste, stir well, and cook, stirring occasionally, for 2 minutes. Pour in 1 cup (240 ml) of the stock and stir to dislodge any browned bits from the pan bottom.

Transfer the contents of the pan to a slow cooker. Add 1 teaspoon salt, several grinds of pepper, and 1 cup (240 ml) stock if you prefer a thicker, more intensely flavored chili, or 2 cups (475 ml) stock if you prefer a soupier chili (for spooning over rice or corn bread). Stir in the browned beef along with any juices. Cover and cook on the low setting for 5 hours. The meat should be very tender.

Just before the chili is ready, make the salsa. Using a large spoon, skim any fat from the surface of the chili. Ladle the chili into shallow individual bowls, top each serving with a heaping spoonful of the salsa, and serve.

BEEF & COCONUT RED CURRY

This Thai-style beef curry comes together quickly when you have coconut milk, red curry paste, and fish sauce already on the pantry shelf. Make the curry a day in advance and its complex flavors will more thoroughly infuse the meat. For a hearty one-pot meal, add a few handfuls of cubed pumpkin or butternut squash along with the beef.

2½ lb (1.1 kg) boneless beef chuck, cut into 1½-inch (4-cm) pieces

Kosher salt and freshly ground pepper

3 tablespoons canola oil

1 yellow onion, finely chopped

4 cloves garlic, minced

¼ cup (60 g) Thai red curry paste

2 cans (14 fl oz/425 ml each) coconut milk (not light), shaken well before opening

2 tablespoons fish sauce

2 tablespoons fresh lime juice

2 tablespoons firmly packed dark brown sugar

3 tablespoons chopped fresh Thai basil or cilantro

SERVES 6–8

Season the beef all over with 1 teaspoon each salt and pepper. In a large, heavy frying pan over medium-high heat, warm the oil. Working in batches if needed to avoid crowding, add the beef and sear, turning as needed, until browned on two sides, 8–10 minutes. Using a slotted spoon, transfer the beef to a plate.

Pour off all but 2 tablespoons of the fat in the pan and return the pan to medium-high heat. Add the onion and garlic and cook, stirring often, until softened, about 6 minutes. Add the curry paste and stir until it is fragrant and evenly coats the onion and garlic, about 30 seconds. Pour in the coconut milk and stir to dislodge the browned bits from the pan bottom. Stir in the fish sauce, lime juice, and sugar and bring to a boil.

Transfer the contents of the pan to a slow cooker and add the beef, stirring to coat evenly. Cover and cook on the low setting for 6 hours or the high setting for 3 hours. The beef should be very tender.

Using a large spoon, skim any fat from the surface of the curry. Spoon the curry onto individual plates or into a serving bowl. Sprinkle with the basil and serve.

Serve this fragrant stew with Crostini (page 176) for sopping up the juices, or spoon the mixture atop thick slices of toasted bread for a hearty midday meal.

FRENCH-STYLE BEEF STEW

No slow cooker book would be complete without a great beef stew recipe. For a colorful spin, swap in multicolored heirloom carrots for the classic variety, or exchange some of the carrots for other root vegetables, such as parsnips or turnips.

½ lb (225 g) applewood smoked bacon, diced

3 lb (1.4 kg) boneless beef chuck, trimmed of excess fat and cut into 2-inch (5-cm) cubes

Kosher salt and freshly ground pepper

¾ cup (90 g) all-purpose flour

2 tablespoons canola oil

4 cloves garlic, smashed

1½ cups (350 ml) dry red wine

1 cup (240 ml) beef or chicken stock

3 fresh thyme sprigs

3 bay leaves

3 large carrots, peeled, halved lengthwise, and cut crosswise into 1-inch (2.5-cm) chunks

½ lb (225 g) cremini mushrooms, brushed clean, stem ends trimmed, and quartered

1 package (10 oz/285 g) frozen pearl onions, thawed and drained

2 tablespoons chopped fresh flat-leaf parsley

SERVES 6

In a large, heavy frying pan over medium heat, cook the bacon, stirring often, until crisp, about 5 minutes. Transfer to a paper towel–lined plate and set aside. Pour off the fat from the pan.

Season the beef generously all over with salt and pepper, then place in a large plastic bag, add the flour, and shake the bag to coat the beef evenly. Remove the meat from the bag and shake off the excess flour.

In the frying pan over medium-high heat, warm the oil. Working in batches if needed to avoid crowding, add the beef and sear, turning as needed, until browned on two sides, 8–10 minutes. Using a slotted spoon, transfer to a slow cooker.

Pour off most of the fat in the pan and return the pan to medium-high heat. Add the garlic and cook, stirring, for about 1 minute. Pour in the wine and stir to dislodge any browned bits from the pan bottom. Add the stock, thyme, and bay leaves, then pour the contents of the pan over the beef. Stir in the carrots. Cover and cook on the low setting for 6 hours.

Add the mushrooms and pearl onions, submerging them in the liquid. Re-cover and continue to cook on the low setting for 1 hour longer. The beef and vegetables should be very tender.

Remove and discard the bay leaves and thyme. Let the stew stand for a few minutes, then use a large spoon to skim the fat from the surface. Ladle the stew into warm shallow bowls, garnish with the parsley, and serve.

BALSAMIC POT ROAST WITH BABY ROOT VEGETABLES

The addition of balsamic vinegar contributes an unexpected sweet tang to the sauce for this hearty pot roast. Look for small or baby vegetables and be sure to cut them into uniform pieces so they cook evenly. If you like your vegetables with a little bite, add them after the pot roast has cooked for 4–5 hours. They will come out crisp-tender.

1 boneless beef chuck roast, 4 lb (1.8 kg), tied

Kosher salt and freshly ground pepper

1 tablespoon canola oil

1 large yellow onion, finely chopped

1 large carrot, peeled and finely chopped

1 large celery stalk, finely chopped

2 cups (475 ml) beef stock

⅓ cup (80 ml) dry red wine

⅓ cup (80 ml) balsamic vinegar

1 tablespoon chopped fresh thyme

¾ lb (340 g) small parsnips, peeled and cut into thick matchsticks

¾ lb (340 g) baby rainbow carrots (2 small bunches), peeled and larger carrots halved lengthwise

½ lb (225 g) baby turnips, peeled and cut into halves or quarters

3 tablespoons unsalted butter

3 tablespoons all-purpose flour

SERVES 6–8

Season the roast generously all over with salt and pepper. In a large, heavy frying pan over medium-high heat, warm the oil. Add the roast and sear, turning as needed, until browned on all sides, about 10 minutes. Using tongs, transfer to a slow cooker.

Pour off all but 1–2 tablespoons of the fat in the pan and return the pan to medium heat. Add the onion, chopped carrot, celery, and ½ teaspoon salt and cook, stirring occasionally, until softened, about 6 minutes. Pour in the stock, wine, and vinegar, add the thyme and another ½ teaspoon salt, then raise the heat to high and bring to a boil, stirring to dislodge any browned bits from the pan bottom. Remove from the heat.

Pour the contents of the pan over the roast. Arrange the parsnips, rainbow carrots, and turnips around the roast, pushing them down into the cooking liquid. Cover and cook on the low setting for 8 hours. The roast and the vegetables should be tender.

Transfer the roast to a cutting board and tent with aluminum foil. Using a slotted spoon, transfer the vegetables to a bowl and cover to keep warm. Strain the cooking liquid into a pitcher or bowl, let stand for a few minutes, then use a large spoon to skim the fat from the surface.

In a saucepan over medium heat, melt the butter. Whisk in the flour, then cook, stirring, for about 1 minute. Slowly add the cooking liquid while whisking constantly, then continue to whisk until thickened to a gravy consistency, about 3 minutes. Taste and adjust the seasoning with salt, pepper, and/or balsamic if needed.

Snip and remove the strings from the roast, then cut the roast against the grain into slices. Transfer the slices to a serving platter and surround them with the vegetables. Spoon some of the gravy over the beef slices and vegetables, then pour the remainder into a small bowl or pitcher. Serve the meat and vegetables with the gravy alongside.

BEER-BRAISED CORNED BEEF & WINTER VEGETABLES

Slow cooking is the best way to coax beef brisket to supple tenderness. In this updated classic, parsnips and carrots add earthy sweetness to the mustard-and-beer–spiked sauce. Serve the flavorful meat and vegetables with warm buttered slices of pain au levain and a full-bodied ale.

1 point-cut corned beef brisket, about 3 lb (1.4 kg), with juices and enclosed spice packet

1 red onion, finely chopped

⅓ cup (60 g) drained sauerkraut

¼ cup (60 g) country Dijon mustard

1 tablespoon firmly packed golden brown sugar

Kosher salt and freshly ground pepper

1½ cups (350 ml) brown or red ale

1 cup (240 ml) chicken stock

1½ lb (680 g) small parsnips or yellow potatoes, peeled and cut into 2-inch (5-cm) pieces

4 carrots, peeled and cut into 2-inch (5-cm) lengths

1 small head green cabbage, cut into 6–8 wedges through the stem end

SERVES 6–8

Put the corned beef and its juices and the contents of the spice packet in a slow cooker. Add the onion, sauerkraut, mustard, sugar, 1 teaspoon salt, and a few grinds of pepper and mix well with your hands. Pour in the ale and stock, then cover and cook on the low setting for 4 hours.

Add the parsnips, carrots, and cabbage wedges, submerging them in the liquid. Re-cover and continue to cook on the low setting for 4–6 hours longer. The vegetables and brisket should be very tender.

Transfer the brisket to a cutting board and let rest for 5 minutes. If you wish to serve the cooking liquid with the brisket, let the liquid stand for a few minutes, then use a large spoon to skim the fat from the surface.

Cut the brisket against the grain into slices. Divide the slices and vegetables among individual plates. If using the warm cooking liquid, spoon some of it over each serving, then serve.

SPRING VEAL STEW WITH LEEKS, ASPARAGUS & PEAS

Choosing quality meat is important, especially when it comes to veal. Grass-fed or meadow veal from a producer with humane raising standards will yield the most flavorful meat. Veal pairs naturally with spring vegetables like grassy asparagus, earthy mushrooms, and sweet, tender peas.

3 lb (1.4 kg) boneless veal shank or shoulder, cut into 2-inch (5-cm) cubes

Kosher salt and freshly ground pepper

3 tablespoons unsalted butter

3 tablespoons olive oil

2 leeks, white and pale green parts, trimmed, halved lengthwise, and thinly sliced crosswise

1 cup (240 ml) dry white wine

2 fresh thyme sprigs

½ lb (225 g) asparagus, tough ends removed and spears cut into 1-inch (2.5-cm) lengths

6 oz (180 g) cremini mushrooms, brushed clean, stem ends trimmed, and sliced

1½ cups (200 g) frozen petite peas

½ cup (120 g) crème fraîche or sour cream

3 tablespoons chopped fresh flat-leaf parsley

SERVES 6–8

Season the veal generously all over with salt and pepper. In a large, heavy frying pan over medium-high heat, melt 2 tablespoons of the butter with 2 tablespoons of the oil. Working in batches if needed to avoid crowding, add the veal and sear, turning as needed, until golden brown on two sides, 8–10 minutes. Add the leeks and cook, stirring, until they start to soften, about 3 minutes longer. Using a slotted spoon, transfer the veal and leeks to a slow cooker.

Return the pan to medium-high heat, pour in the wine, and stir to dislodge the browned bits from the pan bottom. Bring the wine to a boil and pour over the veal and leeks. Add the thyme to the slow cooker, cover, and cook on the low setting for 6 hours. The meat should be very tender.

Just before the veal is ready, in a frying pan over medium heat, melt the remaining 1 tablespoon butter with the remaining 1 tablespoon oil. Add the asparagus, mushrooms, peas, and a pinch of salt and stir to combine. Cover the pan and cook, stirring a few times, until the vegetables are tender, 2–5 minutes.

When the veal is ready, stir in the vegetables. Remove and discard the thyme. Add the crème fraîche, stir to blend well with the cooking juices, and then season with salt and pepper. Spoon the stew into shallow bowls, garnish with the parsley, and serve.

Maple-Bourbon Short Ribs (page 35) with mashed sweet potatoes (page 173)

Stout-Braised Short Ribs (page 34) with sautéed rainbow chard

Adobo-Style Short Ribs (page 34) with Mango Salsa (page 175)

4 WAYS WITH SHORT RIBS

Choose 4 large short ribs for 4 hearty servings or 6 smaller short ribs for 6 servings. Pair the bone-in ribs with steamed rice, mashed potatoes, or fresh greens. You can also remove the meat from the bones, shred it, and make your own bountiful rice or noodle bowls with shredded vegetables or slaw.

Thai-Style Lime & Basil Short Ribs (page 35) with steamed jasmine rice (page 173)

ADOBO-STYLE SHORT RIBS

Season the short ribs with salt and pepper. In a large, heavy frying pan over medium-high heat, warm 2 tablespoons of the oil. Working in batches if needed to avoid crowding, add the ribs and sear, turning as needed, until browned on both sides, 8–10 minutes. Transfer the ribs to a slow cooker in an even layer.

In the same pan over medium heat, warm the reamaining 1 tablespoon oil. Add the onion and carrot and cook, stirring often, until softened, about 6 minutes. Add the garlic, bay leaves, and star anise and cook, stirring, for 1 minute longer. Pour in the vinegar and soy sauce, stir to dislodge any browned bits from the pan bottom, and remove from the heat.

Pour the contents of the pan over the ribs in the slow cooker. Cover and cook on the low setting for 6 hours. The beef should be very tender.

Transfer the ribs to a plate. Strain the cooking liquid into a saucepan. Retrieve the garlic cloves, mash to a paste, and add to the saucepan. Using a large spoon, skim the fat from the surface of the cooking liquid. Bring to a rapid simmer on the stove top over high heat and cook until slightly reduced, about 5 minutes. Meanwhile, remove and discard the bones from the ribs. Shred the meat, transfer to a bowl, and moisten with the reduced cooking liquid. Put the lettuce leaves on a plate, spoon the meat into the leaves, top with the salsa, and serve.

4 lb (1.8 kg) English-cut beef short ribs

Kosher salt and freshly ground pepper

3 tablespoons canola oil

1 yellow onion, finely chopped

1 large carrot, peeled and finely chopped

8 cloves garlic, smashed

2 bay leaves

3 star anise pods

¾ cup (180 ml) rice vinegar

⅓ cup (80 ml) reduced-sodium soy sauce

2 romaine lettuce hearts, leaves separated

Mango Salsa for serving, homemade (page 175) or store-bought

SERVES 4–6

STOUT-BRAISED SHORT RIBS

Season the short ribs with salt and pepper. In a large, heavy frying pan over medium-high heat, warm 2 tablespoons of the oil. Working in batches if needed to avoid crowding, add the ribs and sear, turning as needed, until browned on both sides, 8–10 minutes. Transfer the ribs to a slow cooker in an even layer.

In the same pan over medium heat, warm the remaining 1 tablespoon oil. Add the onions, carrots, celery, and garlic and cook, stirring occasionally, until softened, about 6 minutes. Season with salt and pepper and remove from the heat.

Pour the contents of the pan over the ribs in the slow cooker. Pour in the stout. Cover and cook on the low setting for 6 hours. The beef should be very tender.

Transfer the ribs to a serving platter and keep warm. Let the sauce stand for a few minutes. Using a large spoon, skim the fat from the surface of the sauce. Using an immersion blender, purée the sauce until smooth.

Pour the sauce over the ribs, garnish with the parsley (if using), and serve.

4 lb (1.8 kg) English-cut beef short ribs

Kosher salt and freshly ground pepper

3 tablespoons canola oil

2 yellow onions, finely chopped

3 carrots, peeled and finely chopped

2 celery stalks, diced

6 cloves garlic, sliced

2 cups (480 ml) stout

Chopped flat-leaf parsley sprigs, for garnish (optional)

SERVES 4–6

MAPLE-BOURBON SHORT RIBS

Season the short ribs with salt and pepper. In a large, heavy frying pan over medium-high heat, warm 2 tablespoons of the oil. Working in batches if needed to avoid crowding, add the ribs and sear, turning as needed, until browned on both sides, about 6 minutes. Transfer the ribs to a slow cooker in an even layer.

In the same pan over medium heat, warm the remaining 1 tablespoon oil. Add the onion and cook, stirring often, until slightly caramelized, about 10 minutes. Add the garlic and cook, stirring, for 1 minute. Pour in the bourbon and maple syrup and cook, stirring often, until reduced by half, about 3 minutes. Stir in the stock, rosemary, tomato paste, and Worcestershire sauce. Remove from the heat.

Pour the contents of the pan over the ribs in the slow cooker. Cover and cook on the low setting for 6 hours. The beef should be very tender.

Transfer the ribs to a plate. Strain the cooking liquid into a saucepan. Let stand for a few minutes. Using a large spoon, skim the fat from the surface of the cooking liquid. Place the saucepan on the stove top over medium-high heat, bring to a rapid simmer, and cook until slightly reduced, about 10 minutes.

Spoon the sweet potatoes onto plates, arrange the ribs on top. Drizzle the glaze over the ribs and serve.

4 lb (1.8) boneless beef short ribs

Kosher salt and freshly ground pepper

3 tablespoons olive oil

1 yellow onion, finely chopped

4 cloves garlic, minced

¾ cup (180 ml) bourbon

½ cup (155 g) pure maple syrup

1 cup (240 ml) beef stock

1 tablespoon minced fresh rosemary

1 tablespoon tomato paste

1 tablespoon Worcestershire sauce

Mashed sweet potatoes (page 173), for serving

SERVES 4–6

THAI-STYLE LIME & BASIL SHORT RIBS

Season the short ribs with salt and pepper and put them in a slow cooker in an even layer.

In a bowl, stir together the shallots, garlic, chiles, soy sauce, lime juice, sugar, fish sauce, and half of the basil, mixing well. Pour over the ribs and turn the ribs to coat evenly with the sauce. Tuck the lime leaves into the sauce around the ribs.

Cover and cook on the low setting for 6 hours, turning the ribs once or twice during cooking if possible. The beef should be very tender.

Using tongs, carefully transfer the ribs to a serving platter and keep warm. Remove and discard the lime leaves. Let the sauce stand for a few minutes. Using a large spoon, skim the fat from the surface of the sauce.

Stir the remaining basil into the sauce. Pour the sauce over the ribs and serve.

4 lb (1.8 kg) English-cut beef short ribs

Kosher salt and freshly ground pepper

2 large shallots, finely chopped

4 cloves garlic, minced

2 fresh red Thai chiles, seeded and finely chopped

⅓ cup (80 ml) reduced-sodium soy sauce

⅓ cup (80 ml) fresh lime juice

¼ cup (60 g) firmly packed golden brown sugar

3 tablespoons fish sauce

¼ cup (15 g) chopped fresh Thai basil

4 makrut (kaffir) lime leaves

SERVES 4–6

For a pretty garnish, cut green onions into 3-inch (7.5-cm) pieces, then thinly slice lengthwise. Soak the onion strips in water until curled.

GINGER BEEF UDON NOODLE BOWL WITH SHIITAKE MUSHROOMS

Here, a chuck roast is braised, sliced, then returned to the slow cooker to simmer until perfectly tender. You can also use stew meat—just cut up the chuck roast into 2-inch (5-cm) pieces—which saves the step of slicing the roast midway through cooking (a good option if you are doing this overnight or while at work). To boost the vegetable content, add a few handfuls of baby spinach the last 15 minutes of cooking.

1½ cups (350 ml) beef stock

⅓ cup (80 ml) soy sauce

¼ cup (60 ml) mirin

1 yellow onion, finely chopped

2 tablespoons firmly packed dark brown sugar

2 tablespoons peeled and shredded fresh ginger

1 boneless beef chuck roast, about 3 lb (1.4 kg), tied

Kosher salt and freshly ground pepper

1 tablespoon canola oil

½ lb (225 g) shiitake mushrooms, brushed clean, stems discarded, and caps sliced

1 bunch green onions, including tender green parts, thinly sliced

1½ lb (680 g) dried udon noodles (two 12-oz/340-g packages)

Shichimi togarashi (optional), for garnish

SERVES 8

In a slow cooker, stir together the stock, soy sauce, mirin, onion, brown sugar, and ginger until the sugar dissolves.

Season the roast generously all over with salt and pepper. In a large, heavy frying pan over medium-high to high heat, warm the oil. Add the roast and sear, turning as needed, until browned on all sides, about 10 minutes.

Transfer the roast to the slow cooker, nestling it in the onion mixture. Cover and cook on the low setting for 4 hours.

Transfer the roast to a cutting board and let stand for a couple of minutes, then snip and remove the strings and slice the beef against the grain into thin slices about ¼ inch (6 mm) thick, discarding any large bits of fat.

Stir the mushrooms and half of the green onions into the cooking liquid. Return the beef slices to the slow cooker, re-cover, and cook on the low setting for 3–4 hours. The beef should be very tender.

Just before the beef is ready, bring a large pot three-fourths full of salted water to a boil. Add the udon and boil until tender, according to package directions. Drain, rinse under cold running water, and divide evenly among 8 bowls.

Using a slotted spatula, divide the beef and mushrooms evenly among the bowls. Strain the cooking liquid through a fine-mesh sieve into a bowl, then divide any captured solids among the bowls. Let the cooking liquid stand for a few minutes, then use a large spoon to skim the fat from the surface. Taste the cooking liquid and adjust the seasoning with salt and pepper if needed. If the liquid has cooled, transfer to a small saucepan and reheat on the stove until hot.

Divide the hot cooking liquid evenly among the noodle bowls. Sprinkle with the remaining green onions and the *shichimi togarashi* (if using) and serve.

LASAGNA WITH BEEF RAGÙ, KABOCHA SQUASH & CRÈME FRAÎCHE

If you've never tried making lasagna in a slow cooker, you are in for a treat. Although a few steps are involved, most of them can be done in advance, leaving you only to layer the ingredients directly into the slow cooker and let the lasagna bubble away. If you like, use butternut or other winter squash in place of the kabocha.

1 small kabocha squash, about 1½ lb (680 g)

2 tablespoons olive oil

Kosher salt and freshly ground pepper

1 yellow onion, finely chopped

1 carrot, peeled and finely chopped

2 cloves garlic, minced

1 lb (450 g) lean ground beef

½ lb (225 g) bulk Italian sausage

4 cups (950 ml) marinara sauce

1⅓ cups (320 ml) water

9 dried lasagna noodles (do not use "no-boil" noodles)

1½ cups (340 g) crème fraîche

1 cup (120 g) freshly grated Parmesan cheese

1 cup (120 g) shredded mozzarella cheese

SERVES 8

Preheat the oven to 425°F (220°C). Peel the squash with a vegetable peeler, then halve through the stem end. Using a metal spoon, scoop out and discard the seeds. Cut the squash crosswise into slices ¼ inch (6 mm) thick and transfer to a large rimmed baking sheet. Drizzle with 1 tablespoon of the oil, toss to coat evenly, then spread the slices in a single layer and sprinkle with salt and pepper. Roast until just barely tender when pierced with a fork, about 10 minutes.

Meanwhile, make the beef ragù. In a large frying pan over medium-high heat, warm the remaining 1 tablespoon oil. Add the onion, carrot, garlic, and a pinch of salt and cook, stirring often, until the vegetables have softened, about 6 minutes. Add the beef and sausage and cook, breaking up the meat with a wooden spoon, until the meat is no longer pink, about 10 minutes. Add the marinara sauce and 1 cup (240 ml) of the water, stir well, and bring to a simmer. Remove from the heat.

Spread 2 cups (475 ml) of the sauce on the bottom of the slow cooker. Cover the sauce with 3 uncooked lasagna noodles, breaking the noodles as needed to fit in a single layer. Spread 1 cup (240 ml) of the sauce evenly over the noodles. Dollop ¾ cup (170 g) of the crème fraîche in an even layer on the sauce, then sprinkle with ¼ cup (30 g) of the Parmesan. Arrange half of the squash slices in a single layer over the cheese layer, then top with 1 cup (240 ml) of the sauce. Repeat the layers, starting with 3 noodles, then 1 cup (240 ml) sauce, the remaining ¾ cup (170 g) crème fraîche, ¼ cup (30 g) of the Parmesan, the remaining squash slices, and 1 cup (240 ml) of the sauce. Top the sauce with a third layer of noodles, then the remaining sauce (about 1½ cups/350 ml). Top evenly with the mozzarella and the remaining ½ cup (60 g) Parmesan. Drizzle the remaining ⅓ cup (80 ml) water around the edges of the lasagna.

Cover and cook on the low setting for 4 hours. The lasagna noodles and squash will be cooked through and tender.

Uncover, taking care not to let the condensation on the lid drip back onto the lasagna. Let stand for 10 minutes before serving directly from the slow cooker.

SLOW-COOKED BEEF BOLOGNESE WITH PAPPARDELLE

Long, slow cooking at a low temperature transforms ground beef, tomatoes, and a handful of other everyday ingredients into a sumptuous Bolognese sauce. Serve it tossed with *pappardelle*, as it is here, or with another pasta shape; use it in lasagna or another baked pasta; or spoon it over Creamy Polenta (page 173).

½ lb (225 g) applewood-smoked bacon or pancetta, diced

1 large yellow onion, finely chopped

2 carrots, peeled and finely chopped

2 celery stalks, finely chopped

Kosher salt and freshly ground pepper

2 cloves garlic, minced

1½ lb (680 g) lean ground beef

1½ lb (680 g) ground pork

½ cup (120 ml) whole milk

1 can (28 oz/800 g) crushed tomatoes with juices

1 cup (240 ml) beef stock

½ cup (120 ml) full-bodied red wine

1 lb (450 g) fresh pappardelle or fettuccine

½ cup (60 g) freshly shaved or grated Parmesan cheese

SERVES 4–6, WITH LEFTOVER SAUCE

In a large, heavy frying pan over medium heat, cook the bacon, stirring often, until crisp, about 5 minutes. Add the onion, carrots, celery, 1 teaspoon salt, and a few grinds of pepper and cook, stirring often, until softened, about 6 minutes. Stir in the garlic, then stir in the beef and pork and cook, stirring and breaking up the meats with a wooden spoon, until they are no longer pink, about 5 minutes. Stir in the milk and cook, stirring occasionally, for 2 minutes. Pour in the tomatoes and their juices, stock, and the wine and stir until blended. Bring the sauce to a boil and remove from the heat.

Transfer the contents of the pan to a slow cooker, cover, and cook on the low setting for 8 hours. Using a large spoon, skim any fat from the surface of the sauce. The sauce should be thick and the flavors blended. Taste and adjust the seasoning with salt and pepper.

About 15 minutes before the sauce is ready, bring a large pot three-fourths full of salted water to a boil. Add the pasta and cook until al dente, 2–4 minutes. Drain the pasta and return it to the pot. Add about ½ cup (120 ml) of the sauce and toss gently to coat.

Divide the pasta among shallow individual bowls and top with additional sauce, using about half of the remaining sauce. Sprinkle a little of the Parmesan over each portion and serve. Pass the remaining cheese at the table. Let the remaining sauce cool to room temperature, then transfer to an airtight container and refrigerate for up to 4 days or freeze for up to 3 months.

BEEF STROGANOFF WITH WILD MUSHROOMS

Stroganoff is indeed a traditional dish, but the addition of wild mushrooms, or even a medley of mixed, cultivated mushrooms, adds both interest and flavor. Plenty of fresh herbs bring a bright note. Serve with egg noodles for a classic presentation, or atop a bed of steamed spinach for a lighter offering.

7 tablespoons all-purpose flour

Kosher salt and freshly ground pepper

8 tablespoons (4 oz/115 g) unsalted butter

3 tablespoons olive oil

3 lb (1.4 kg) boneless beef chuck, cut crosswise into strips about ½ inch (12 mm) wide

1 yellow onion, thinly sliced

2 cloves garlic, minced

1 cup (8 fl oz/240 ml) dry red wine

2 cups (16 fl oz/475 ml) beef broth

2 sprigs fresh thyme

1½ lb (680 g) assorted fresh, wild mushrooms, brushed clean, stems removed, and cut into bite-size pieces if needed

¼ cup (2 fl oz/60 ml) dry sherry

2 tablespoons Worcestershire sauce

1½ teaspoons dry mustard

2 cups (18 fl oz/500 ml) sour cream

1 lb (450 g) wide egg noodles

2 tablespoons chopped fresh flat-leaf parsley

SERVES 6

In a bowl, stir together 3 tablespoons of the flour, 1 teaspoon salt, and 1 teaspoon pepper. In a large, heavy frying pan over medium-high heat, melt 2 tablespoons of the butter with 2 tablespoons of the oil. Working in batches, roll the beef strips in the seasoned flour and cook, turning occasionally, until browned on two sides, about 5 minutes. Transfer to a slow cooker.

Add the onion to the pan and cook, stirring, over medium-high heat until softened, about 6 minutes. Add the garlic and sauté for about 30 seconds. Add the wine and broth and bring to a boil, stirring and scraping up the browned bits on the pan bottom with a wooden spoon.

Pour the onion mixture over the beef and add the thyme. Cover and cook until the beef is tender, 6 hours on the low setting or 3 hours on the high setting.

In a large frying pan over medium heat, melt 4 tablespoons butter with the remaining 1 tablespoon oil. Add the mushrooms and a pinch of salt and cook, stirring, until they begin to brown, about 4 minutes. Sprinkle with the remaining 4 tablespoons flour and stir to coat evenly. Stir in the sherry, Worcestershire sauce, and mustard until thoroughly blended, then stir in the sour cream. Add to the beef mixture, stirring to combine evenly. Cover and continue to cook on the low setting until warmed through, about 15 minutes.

Meanwhile, cook the egg noodles in a large pot of boiling salted water until tender, according to package directions. Drain and transfer to a large serving bowl. Add the remaining 2 tablespoons butter to the noodles and toss to coat, then season with salt and pepper. Spoon the beef and mushroom sauce over the noodles, garnish with the parsley, and serve.

For individual potpies, spoon the beef and mushroom filling into ramekins, cut the pie dough to fit, and bake as directed.

BEEF & MUSHROOM POTPIE

Let the braised beef and vegetable filling simmer overnight or while you are at work, then just pop it into a baking dish, cover with store-bought pie dough, and bake for 30 minutes. Your guests will think you spent all day creating this comfort-food favorite.

½ cup (60 g) all-purpose flour, plus more for dusting the work surface

Kosher salt and freshly ground pepper

2½ lb (1.1 kg) boneless beef chuck, cut into 2-inch (5-cm) chunks

2 tablespoons canola oil, or as needed

½ lb (225 g) fresh cremini mushrooms, brushed clean, stem ends trimmed, and thickly sliced

3 tablespoons unsalted butter

1 yellow onion, finely chopped

1 large or 2 medium carrots, peeled and finely chopped

1 large celery stalk, finely chopped

1 teaspoon dried thyme

1 teaspoon dried oregano

2 tablespoons tomato paste

1 cup (240 ml) lager-style beer

1½ cups (350 ml) beef stock

½ lb (225 g) store-bought frozen all-butter pie dough, thawed according to package directions

SERVES 6–8

On a rimmed plate, stir together ¼ cup (30 g) of the flour, 1 teaspoon salt, and ½ teaspoon pepper. Working in batches, roll the beef chunks in the flour mixture, coating evenly and shaking off the excess. In a large, heavy frying pan over medium-high heat, warm the oil. Working in batches if needed to avoid crowding, add the beef and sear, turning as needed, until browned on two sides, about 10 minutes. (If frying in batches, add more oil, by the tablespoon, if needed.) Using a slotted spoon, transfer to a slow cooker. When all of the beef is browned, add the mushrooms to the slow cooker and stir to combine.

Return the pan to medium heat and melt the butter. Add the onion, carrots, celery, and 1 teaspoon salt and cook, stirring occasionally, until the onion begins to brown, about 6 minutes. Stir in the thyme and oregano. Sprinkle the remaining ¼ cup (30 g) flour over the vegetables and stir to coat evenly. Stir in the tomato paste. Slowly add the beer followed by the stock while stirring constantly, then continue to stir until the mixture thickens, about 1 minute.

Pour the vegetable mixture over the beef and mushrooms (the combined ingredients will look fairly dry, but the mushrooms will release quite a bit of liquid). Cover and cook on the low setting for 6 hours, stirring once halfway during cooking if possible. The meat should be very tender.

Using tongs, transfer the beef pieces to a cutting board. Using 2 forks, shred the beef into bite-size pieces, removing any large bits of fat. Using a large spoon, skim the fat from the surface of the cooking liquid. Return the meat to the slow cooker and cover to keep warm.

Preheat the oven to 400°F (200°C). Lightly dust a work surface with flour, then roll out the pie dough into a round about 12 inches (30 cm) in diameter and ⅛-inch (3 mm) thick. Cut a few vents into the center of the dough.

Pour the beef mixture into a 9½-inch (24-cm) deep-dish pie dish. Place the dish on a baking sheet. Lay the dough round over the warm filling, trim any excess overhang, and then crimp the edges decoratively. Bake the potpie until the crust is golden brown, about 30 minutes. Serve hot.

FRENCH DIP SANDWICHES WITH CARAMELIZED ONIONS

Slow-cooking pot roast on a bed of caramelized onions makes for wonderfully tender meat and exceptionally rich and flavorful juices for dipping these delectable sandwiches. Melted provolone cheese adds the finishing touch.

FOR THE CARAMELIZED ONIONS

3 large yellow onions, halved and thinly sliced

3 tablespoons unsalted butter, melted

Kosher salt

1½ cups (350 ml) beef stock

¼ cup (60 ml) dry red wine

2 bay leaves

1 boneless beef chuck roast, about 4 lb (1.8 kg), tied

Kosher salt and freshly ground pepper

1 tablespoon canola oil

8 crusty French sandwich rolls, split and toasted

¾ lb (340 g) sliced provolone cheese (8 slices)

SERVES 8

To make the caramelized onions, the night before serving, put the onions in a slow cooker, add the butter and ½ teaspoon salt, and toss to coat evenly. Cover and cook on the low setting for 10 hours, stirring once in the first few hours of cooking if possible. The next morning, stir the onions, re-cover, and cook on the high setting until the onions are golden and most of the liquid has evaporated, 1–2 hours. If the liquid has not evaporated, set the lid ajar for 1–2 hours to evaporate the liquid while the onions continue to cook. (The onions can be caramelized in advance. Let cool to room temperature, then transfer to an airtight container and refrigerate for up to 3 days or freeze for up to 3 months.)

When the onions are ready, stir in the stock, wine, and bay leaves.

Season the roast with salt and pepper. In a large, heavy frying pan over medium-high heat, warm the oil. Add the roast and sear, turning as needed, until browned on all sides, about 10 minutes. Transfer the roast to the slow cooker, nestling it in the onion mixture. Cover and cook on the low setting for 4 hours.

Transfer the roast to a cutting board and let stand for a couple of minutes, then snip and remove the strings and cut the roast against the grain into slices about ¼ inch (6 mm) thick, discarding any large bits of fat. Return the sliced beef to the slow cooker, re-cover, and continue to cook on the low setting for 4 hours. The beef should be very tender.

Using a slotted spatula, carefully transfer the beef slices and onions to a platter. Strain the cooking juices through a fine-mesh sieve into a serving bowl. Transfer any onions captured in the sieve to the platter and discard the bay leaves. Let the cooking juices stand for a few minutes. Using a large spoon, skim the fat from the surface of the juices. Taste the juices and adjust the seasoning with salt and pepper if needed, then keep warm.

To assemble the sandwiches, pile slices of beef and onions onto the bottom half of each roll, dividing them evenly (about 5 oz/140 g meat per roll), then top with a slice of provolone. Close with the roll tops and serve, with bowls of the warm cooking juices alongside for dipping.

Make this sumptuous sandwich in two parts: first caramelize the onions overnight, then slow-cook the beef chuck roast with the onions the next day.

PICADILLO TOSTADAS WITH VEGETABLE SLAW

Picadillo, a finely cut mixture of beef, tomato, olives, raisins, and spices, turns up in many guises throughout the Caribbean and Latin America and is also a staple of the Tex-Mex table. It is used as a topping here, but makes a piquant filling for crispy taco shells, too. For a healthier version, forgo the tortillas in favor of lettuce cups.

1½ lb (680 g) boneless beef chuck, trimmed of excess fat and cut into ½-inch (12-mm) cubes

Kosher salt and freshly ground pepper

2 tablespoons canola oil, plus more for frying

1 yellow onion, finely chopped

3 cloves garlic, finely chopped

2 small Granny Smith or other tart green apples, peeled, cored, and coarsely grated

1 cup (250 g) canned crushed tomatoes

2 tablespoons cider vinegar

3 bay leaves

2 teaspoons ground cumin

2 teaspoons dried oregano

¼ teaspoon ground cinnamon

⅓ cup (55 g) golden raisins

Vegetable Slaw (page 174) or shredded cabbage, for serving

½ cup (60 g) slivered almonds, toasted and chopped

½ cup (70 g) sliced pimiento-stuffed green olives

6–12 corn tostadas

2–3 tablespoons coarsely chopped fresh cilantro

SERVES 6

Season the beef generously all over with salt and pepper. In a large, heavy frying pan over medium-high heat, warm the 2 tablespoons oil. Working in batches if necessary to avoid crowding, add the beef and sear, turning as needed, until browned on two sides, about 10 minutes. Using a slotted spoon, transfer the beef to a slow cooker.

Pour off most of the fat in the pan and return the pan to medium heat. Add the onion and cook, stirring occasionally, until softened, about 6 minutes. Add the garlic and cook, stirring, for about 1 minute longer. Transfer the contents of the pan to the slow cooker.

Stir in the apples, tomatoes, vinegar, bay leaves, cumin, oregano, cinnamon, raisins, ½ teaspoon salt, and several grinds of pepper. Cover and cook on the low setting for 5 hours, stirring once halfway during cooking if possible. The meat should be very tender.

Make the vegetable slaw and set aside.

Using a slotted spoon, transfer the meat and vegetables to a serving bowl. Remove and discard the bay leaves, then keep warm. Let the cooking liquid stand for a few minutes. Using a large spoon, skim the fat from the surface of the cooking liquid. Add just enough of the liquid to the meat to make it juicy and discard the remainder. Fold in the almonds and olives and keep warm.

To serve, top the tostadas with the picadillo, a generous spoonful of the slaw, and some of the cilantro.

THAI-STYLE BRISKET WITH PINEAPPLE RELISH

Braised with garlic, lemongrass, and soy sauce, this brisket is terrific straight out of the slow cooker. But if you top it with a colorful pineapple relish that's been amplified by sweet chile sauce and briny fish sauce, the meal becomes something special. Serve the brisket over steamed rice (page 173) or Zucchini Noodles (page 174).

1 point-cut beef brisket, about 2 lb (900 g), trimmed of excess fat

Kosher salt and freshly ground pepper

2 tablespoons olive oil

1 large yellow onion, coarsely chopped

1 carrot, peeled and coarsely chopped

5 cloves garlic, smashed

1 lemongrass stalk, bulb portion only, tough outer leaves removed and thinly sliced (optional)

¼ cup (60 ml) dry white wine

½ cup (120 ml) chicken or beef stock

¼ cup (60 ml) soy sauce

FOR THE PINEAPPLE RELISH

1 cup (170 g) finely diced fresh or drained canned pineapple

2 tablespoons finely diced red bell pepper

1 tablespoon minced red onion

2 teaspoons soy sauce

1½ teaspoons fish sauce

1 teaspoon Thai sweet chile sauce

6 fresh mint leaves, minced

1 teaspoon minced fresh cilantro

SERVES 6

Season the brisket generously all over with salt and pepper. In a large, heavy frying pan over medium-high heat, warm the oil. Add the brisket and sear, turning once, until browned on both sides, about 10 minutes. Transfer the brisket to a plate.

Pour off most of the fat in the pan and return the pan to medium-high heat. Add the onion and carrot and cook, stirring often, until softened, about 6 minutes. Add the garlic and lemongrass (if using) and cook, stirring, for about 1 minute longer. Pour in the wine and stir to dislodge any browned bits from the pan bottom. Stir in the stock, soy sauce, and several grinds of pepper.

Transfer the contents of the pan to a slow cooker and place the brisket and any accumulated juices on top. Cover and cook on the low setting for 9 hours. The brisket should be very tender.

Up to 4 hours before the brisket is ready, make the relish. In a bowl, toss together the pineapple, bell pepper, onion, soy sauce, fish sauce, chile sauce, mint, and cilantro, mixing well. Set aside if serving right away, or cover and refrigerate for up to 4 hours.

Transfer the brisket to a cutting board and let rest for 5 minutes. Strain the cooking liquid through a fine-mesh sieve, discarding the solids. Let the liquid stand for a few minutes. Using a large spoon, skim the fat from the surface of the liquid.

Cut the brisket against the grain into thick slices, removing any large pieces of fat. Divide the slices among individual plates. Spoon some of the cooking liquid over the slices, spoon the relish over the top, and serve.

PORK & LAMB

BÁNH MÌ RICE BOWL

Pork *bánh mì* is a popular Vietnamese sandwich of marinated grilled pork topped with pickled carrots, cucumber, daikon, cilantro, chiles, and a splash of fish sauce. Here, the pork is slowly cooked with Vietnamese-style seasonings until tender, then served over rice with a sweet-tangy-spicy sauce and plenty of pickled vegetables.

Tangy Dipping Sauce (page 175)

FOR THE PICKLED VEGETABLES

2 large carrots, peeled

1 daikon radish, peeled

½ cup (120 ml) rice vinegar

2 tablespoons sugar

Kosher salt

FOR THE PORK

¼ cup (60 g) firmly packed golden brown sugar

6 cloves garlic, minced

2 large shallots, finely chopped

2 lemongrass stalks, tough outer layers removed, bulb portion only, and minced

3 tablespoons soy sauce

3 tablespoons fish sauce

Juice of 1 lime

½ teaspoon freshly ground pepper

3 lb (1.4 kg) boneless pork shoulder

1 cup (240 ml) chicken stock

Steamed White Rice (page 173), for serving

Fresh cilantro leaves, thinly sliced cucumber, and thinly sliced jalapeño, for serving

SERVES 8

Make the dipping sauce and set aside.

To make the pickled vegetables, cut the carrots and daikon into matchsticks. In a frying pan over medium-high heat, combine the vinegar, sugar, and ¼ teaspoon salt and bring to a boil, stirring until the sugar dissolves. Add the carrots and daikon and toss to combine (a pair of tongs is a good tool for this). Return to a boil and boil for 30 seconds. Remove from the heat and set aside to cool to room temperature, stirring occasionally. Transfer to an airtight container and refrigerate for up to 3 days.

To prepare the pork, in a small bowl, mix the sugar, garlic, shallots, lemongrass, soy sauce, fish sauce, lime juice, and pepper. Trim the pork shoulder of excess fat and cut the meat into 4 equal pieces. Place the pork pieces in a large lock-top plastic bag, add the marinade, and seal the bag closed. Turn the bag over a few times to coat the pork evenly with the marinade, then refrigerate overnight.

The next day, transfer the pork and marinade to a slow cooker. Pour in the stock, cover, and cook on the low setting for 6 hours. The pork should be very tender.

Transfer the pork to a platter. Using 2 forks, pull the pork into shreds, removing and discarding any large bits of fat. Strain the cooking liquid through a fine-mesh sieve into a small bowl. Let stand for a few minutes, then use a large spoon to skim the fat from the surface.

To assemble, divide the rice evenly among 8 large bowls. Top with the pork, dividing it evenly and moistening it with some of the cooking liquid. Top each serving with an equal amount of the pickled vegetables, cilantro, cucumber, and jalapeño slices. Serve the sauce alongside.

TAMARIND-GLAZED PORK SPARERIBS

These sticky-sweet ribs start with a long braise in a slow cooker, then take a quick turn under the broiler, where the sauce perfectly glazes each rib. Tamarind gives the sauce a rich, dark, tangy-sweet flavor. If you have a mandoline, use it to shave the vegetables paper-thin. Serve the ribs with steamed rice (page 173) or roasted yams (page 174).

4 lb (1.8 kg) pork spareribs

Kosher salt and freshly ground pepper

Grated zest of 1 orange

1 cup (240 ml) fresh orange juice

¼ cup (60 g) firmly packed golden brown sugar

2 tablespoons peeled and shredded fresh ginger

5 star anise pods

1 jalapeño chile, seeded, if desired, and finely chopped

⅓ cup (90 g) tamarind paste

⅓ cup (75 g) ketchup

⅓ cup (80 ml) cider vinegar

1 tablespoon honey

1 tablespoon reduced-sodium soy sauce

½ English cucumber, very thinly sliced

¼ small red onion, very thinly sliced

¼ cup (15 g) chopped fresh cilantro leaves

Juice of ½ lime

Lime wedges, for serving

SERVES 6

Cut the ribs into 2-bone portions. Season them generously all over with salt and pepper. In a slow cooker, whisk together the orange zest, orange juice, brown sugar, ginger, star anise, and chile until the sugar dissolves. Add the ribs and turn to coat evenly. Cover and cook on the low setting for 6 hours. The ribs should be tender.

Preheat the broiler. Using tongs, transfer the ribs to a rimmed baking sheet and reserve. Pour the cooking liquid through a fine-mesh sieve set over a bowl. Let the liquid stand for a few minutes. Using a large spoon, skim the fat from the surface of the cooking liquid.

To make the sauce for glazing, pour ¾ cup (180 ml) of the cooking liquid into a small, heavy saucepan. Add the tamarind paste, ketchup, vinegar, honey, and soy sauce, and whisk to combine. Place over medium heat, bring to a simmer, and cook, stirring often, until the sauce thickens to a syrupy consistency, about 8 minutes.

Brush each rib piece generously with the sauce, coating both sides completely. Transfer any remaining sauce to a bowl. Broil the ribs, turning once, until sticky and browned, about 2 minutes. Transfer the ribs to a platter.

In a bowl, toss together the cucumber, onion, cilantro, lime juice, and a pinch of salt. Scatter the cucumber mixture over the ribs or serve alongside. Serve with the lime wedges and the remaining sauce.

BABY BACK RIBS
WITH BARBECUE SAUCE

Sure, baby back ribs are amazing when cooked in a backyard smoker, which you must closely tend for hours. Or you can put them in a slow cooker, walk away, and then return several hours later to fall-off-the-bone goodness. The ribs do benefit from a quick trip under the broiler to crisp up the edges, so don't forget that step.

FOR THE BARBECUE SAUCE

1 tablespoon bacon drippings or canola oil

½ yellow onion, finely chopped

3 cloves garlic, minced

1 cup (225 g) ketchup

3 tablespoons Worcestershire sauce

3 tablespoons dry white wine

½ teaspoon grated lemon zest

1½ tablespoons fresh lemon juice

1½ tablespoons firmly packed dark brown sugar

1½ teaspoons dry mustard

1½ teaspoons chipotle chile powder

1 teaspoon ground cumin

¼ teaspoon celery salt

Kosher salt

1 teaspoon hot-pepper sauce such as Tabasco, or to taste

5 lb (2.3 kg) baby back ribs

SERVES 6

To make the barbecue sauce, in a large, heavy saucepan over medium heat, warm the bacon drippings. Add the onion and garlic and cook until softened, about 6 minutes. Stir in the ketchup, Worcestershire sauce, wine, lemon zest and juice, brown sugar, mustard, chile powder, cumin, celery salt, and ½ teaspoon salt. Bring to a simmer, then reduce the heat to low and cook gently, stirring occasionally to prevent scorching, until slightly thickened, about 12 minutes. Stir in the hot-pepper sauce, then taste and adjust the seasoning with salt and hot-pepper sauce if needed. Use right away, or let cool, cover, and refrigerate for 24 hours before using to develop the flavors.

Preheat the broiler. Place a wire rack in a large rimmed baking sheet. Remove the membrane from the back of each rib rack: at one corner, slide a knife between the membrane and bone to lift and loosen the membrane, then, with a paper towel, grasp the edge of it and pull it free of the rack. Cut the racks into individual ribs. Arrange the ribs on the wire rack and broil, turning once, until browned on both sides, 10–12 minutes.

Transfer the ribs to a slow cooker, add the barbecue sauce, and turn the ribs to coat evenly. Cover and cook on the low setting for 6 hours. The ribs should be very tender.

Using a slotted spatula, transfer the ribs to a large serving platter and keep warm. Pour the sauce into a small, heavy saucepan, let stand for a few minutes, then use a large spoon to skim the fat from the surface. Bring the sauce to a boil over high heat and boil rapidly to reduce and thicken slightly, 3–4 minutes. Drizzle the ribs with some of the reduced sauce and serve.

GARLICKY PORK & KALE WITH WHITE BEAN SALAD

Sturdy pork shoulder becomes tender, juicy, and flavorful when cooked at a low temperature with ample seasonings. Garlic is the star of the show in this recipe and a natural sidekick to both the pork and the greens. Serve this simple yet satisfying main with country-style bread or mashed (page 173) or roasted (page 174) potatoes.

2½ lb (1.1 kg) boneless pork shoulder, trimmed of excess fat and cut into 1½-inch (4-cm) chunks

Kosher salt and freshly ground pepper

2 tablespoons olive oil

1 large yellow onion, finely chopped

2 fresh thyme sprigs

15–20 cloves garlic

1 teaspoon minced fresh rosemary (optional)

⅔ cup (160 ml) dry red wine

1 tablespoon red wine vinegar

⅔ cup (160 ml) beef or chicken stock

About 1¼ lb (570 g) kale, tough stems removed and leaves cut crosswise into wide strips

FOR THE BEAN SALAD

1 can (15 oz/425 g) cannellini beans, rinsed and drained

3 tablespoons extra-virgin olive oil

1 tablespoon red wine vinegar

2 tablespoons finely chopped fresh flat-leaf parsley

¼ red onion, very thinly sliced

Kosher salt and freshly ground pepper

SERVES 6

Season the pork generously all over with salt and pepper. In a large, heavy frying pan over medium-high heat, warm the oil. Working in batches if needed to avoid crowding, add the pork and sear, turning as needed, until browned on two sides, about 10 minutes. Using a slotted spoon, transfer the pork to a plate.

Pour off most of the fat in the pan and return the pan to medium-high heat. Add the onion and thyme and cook, stirring often, until the onion is lightly golden, about 6 minutes. Add the garlic and rosemary and cook, stirring, for 1 minute longer. Pour in the wine and vinegar and stir to dislodge any browned bits from the pan bottom.

Transfer the contents of the pan to a slow cooker. Add the stock and the pork and stir to mix well. Cover and cook on the low setting for 6 hours. Stir in the kale, re-cover, and cook for 30–60 minutes longer. The pork and kale should be very tender.

Meanwhile, make the white bean salad. In a bowl, combine the beans, oil, vinegar, parsley, onion, ¼ teaspoon salt, and several grinds of pepper and stir well. Taste and adjust the seasoning with salt and pepper. Cover and set aside until ready to serve.

When the pork is ready, using the slotted spoon, divide the pork and kale among individual plates. Let the cooking liquid stand for a few minutes, then use a large spoon to skim the fat from the surface. Drizzle some of the liquid over the pork to moisten it, then top each serving with a large spoonful of the bean salad and serve.

This meaty sauce is best
paired with sturdy pasta
shapes. Try gemelli (as here),
penne, orrechiette, bucatini,
or your own favorite.

PORK SHOULDER, PANCETTA & HERB RAGÙ WITH PENNE

Move over Bolognese. This mix of tender pork shoulder and tomato sauce, flavored with pancetta and a trio of herbs, is destined to become your new go-to sauce. It is delicious tossed with penne or gemelli (as here), or serve it atop spiralized zucchini or a pile of sautéed greens (both on page 174), or even Creamy Polenta (page 173).

1 tablespoon olive oil

½ lb (225 g) thickly sliced pancetta or thick-cut bacon, diced

1 large yellow onion, finely chopped

2 carrots, peeled and finely chopped

4 large cloves garlic, minced

Kosher salt and freshly ground pepper

1 can (6 oz/170 g) tomato paste

½ cup (120 ml) dry red wine

1 can (28 oz/800 g) crushed tomatoes

1 can (14½ oz/410 g) diced tomatoes with juices

2 tablespoons chopped fresh flat-leaf Italian parsley, plus more for garnish

2 teaspoons chopped fresh oregano

2 teaspoons chopped fresh thyme

3 lb (1.4 kg) boneless pork shoulder, trimmed of excess fat and cut into 4 equal pieces

1 lb (450 g) gemelli pasta

Freshly grated Parmesan, for garnish

SERVES 6–8, PLUS LEFTOVER SAUCE

In a large frying pan over medium-high heat, warm the oil. Add the pancetta and cook, stirring often, until lightly browned, about 3 minutes. Add the onion, carrots, garlic, and 1 teaspoon salt and cook, stirring often, until the vegetables have softened, about 6 minutes. Stir in the tomato paste, followed by the wine, and then add the crushed tomatoes, diced tomatoes and their juices, parsley, oregano, and thyme, and stir to mix well. Bring to a simmer and remove from the heat.

Pour the tomato mixture into a slow cooker, then add the pork and submerge it in the mixture. Cover and cook on the low setting for 6 hours. The pork should be very tender.

Transfer the pork to a cutting board. Using 2 forks, pull the pork into shreds, removing and discarding any large bits of fat. Let the tomato sauce stand for a few minutes, then use a large spoon to skim the fat from the surface. Return the shredded pork to the sauce, cover, and cook on the low setting for 15 minutes to warm through. You should have about 9 cups (2 l) sauce.

While the sauce is warming, bring a large pot three-fourths full of salted water to a boil over high heat. Add the pasta and cook until al dente, according to package directions. Drain and transfer to a shallow serving bowl.

Add about half of the sauce to the pasta (enough to coat it well) and toss to coat evenly. Garnish with Parmesan and parsley and serve. Let the remaining sauce cool to room temperature, then transfer to 1 or more airtight containers and refrigerate for up to 3 days or freeze for up to 3 months.

PULLED PORK SLIDERS WITH SPICY SLAW

A pot of fork-tender pulled pork is perfect for a big gathering of friends and family. Keep the pork warm in the slow cooker until ready to serve, then set it out buffet-style with a basket of soft buns and a bowl of spicy coleslaw for building the sliders, plus sides of baked beans and potato salad from your favorite deli.

3 lb (1.4 kg) boneless pork shoulder

Kosher salt and freshly ground pepper

2 tablespoons canola oil

1 yellow onion, finely chopped

2 cloves garlic, minced

½ cup (120 ml) chicken stock

2 cups (475 ml) good-quality store-bought barbecue sauce

3 tablespoons yellow mustard

FOR THE SPICY SLAW

½ head green cabbage, cored and thinly sliced crosswise

½ small red onion, very thinly sliced

1 carrot, peeled and shredded

1 tablespoon cider vinegar

¾ cup (180 ml) mayonnaise

1–2 teaspoons Sriracha sauce

Kosher salt and freshly ground pepper

12 slider buns, split and warmed

Barbecue sauce, for serving

SERVES 6

Trim the pork of excess fat and cut the meat into 4 equal pieces. Season the pork generously all over with salt and pepper. In a large, heavy frying pan over medium-high heat, warm the oil. Working in batches if necessary, add the pork and sear, turning as needed, until browned on two sides, about 10 minutes. Transfer the pork to a slow cooker.

Pour off all but 2 tablespoons of the fat in the pan and return the pan to medium-high heat. Add the onion and cook, stirring often, until softened, about 6 minutes. Add the garlic and cook, stirring, for about 1 minute. Pour in the stock and stir to dislodge the browned bits from the pan bottom. Season with salt and pepper, then pour over the pork in the slow cooker. Cover and cook on the low setting for 6 hours. The pork should be very tender.

At least 2 hours before serving, make the slaw. In a large bowl, combine the cabbage, onion, and carrot. Sprinkle with the vinegar and toss to coat evenly. Add the mayonnaise and Sriracha to taste and mix well. Season with salt and pepper. Transfer to a serving bowl, cover, and refrigerate until chilled, at least 2 hours or for up to 1 day.

Transfer the pork to a platter and let cool slightly. Discard any remaining cooking liquid. Using 2 forks, pull the pork into shreds, removing and discarding any large bits of fat.

Return the shredded pork to the slow cooker. Add the barbecue sauce and mustard, season with salt and pepper, and stir to mix well. Cook uncovered on the high setting, stirring a few times, until the flavors are well blended and the sauce has thickened, about 30 minutes.

Spoon the pork and its sauce into a serving bowl, or keep warm on low and serve directly from the cooker. Offer the buns at the table for diners to fill with the pork and slaw. Pass additional barbecue sauce at the table, if desired.

Chewy, soft pretzel rolls
add updated personality
to these flavor-packed
pork sliders.

HAWAIIAN-STYLE KALUA PORK RICE BOWLS WITH PINEAPPLE

Traditional kalua pork is rubbed with salt and slowly roasted in an *imu*, an underground oven that infuses the meat with smoke. You can replicate the shredded tender pork in your slow cooker by using coarse salt and liquid smoke.

3½–4 lb (1.6–1.8 kg) boneless pork shoulder, trimmed of excess fat and cut into 4 equal pieces

2 tablespoons alaea (Hawaiian) salt or coarse sea salt

2 tablespoons canola oil

1 teaspoon liquid smoke

1 pineapple

3 tablespoons firmly packed golden brown sugar

Steamed rice (page 173), for serving

SERVES 6–8

Using a paring knife, pierce the pork all over, then rub the pork with the salt. In a large, heavy frying pan over medium-high heat, warm the oil. Working in batches if needed to avoid crowding, add the pork and sear, turning as needed, until evenly browned on all sides, about 10 minutes. Using tongs, transfer the pork to a slow cooker.

Sprinkle the pork all over with the liquid smoke, then cover and cook on the low setting for 8–10 hours. The pork should be very tender.

Meanwhile, trim off both ends from the pineapple, then cut away the peel, including the "eyes." Cut the pineapple crosswise into 10–12 slices. Using a small round biscuit cutter or a sharp knife, cut out the core from the center of each slice.

Place a rack in the upper third of the oven and preheat the broiler. Arrange the pineapple in a single layer on a rimmed baking sheet. Sprinkle the slices evenly with the brown sugar. Broil until golden brown, about 2 minutes. Remove from the broiler and leave the slices whole or chop roughly, then set aside until ready to use.

Transfer the pork to a cutting board. Using 2 forks, pull the pork into shreds, removing and discarding any large bits of fat. Transfer the pork to a serving bowl. Using a large spoon, skim the fat from the surface of the cooking liquid. Moisten the shredded pork with some of the warm liquid.

Spoon the rice into large individual bowls, top with the pork and pineapple, and serve.

PORK RAMEN WITH GINGER & SHIITAKE MUSHROOMS

Traditional Japanese pork ramen can take days to make. This simplified version simmers in a slow cooker throughout the day to create a deeply flavored broth and succulent meat. A runny egg slipped into each bowl adds silky richness to the soup.

3 lb (1.4 kg) boneless pork shoulder, trimmed of excess fat, cut into 4 equal pieces

Kosher salt

2 tablespoons canola oil

1 yellow onion, coarsely chopped

6 cloves garlic, chopped

2-inch (5-cm) piece fresh ginger, peeled and chopped

8 cups (64 fl oz/1.9 l) chicken stock

1 leek, white and green parts, halved lengthwise and coarsely chopped

¼ lb (120 g) shiitake mushrooms, brushed clean and coarsely chopped

Reduced-sodium soy sauce, for seasoning

Sesame and/or chile oil, for seasoning

1½ lb (750 g) fresh ramen noodles

8 large eggs (optional)

About 4 green onions, white and tender green parts, finely chopped

SERVES 8

Season the pork with salt. In a large, heavy frying pan over medium-high heat, warm the oil. Working in batches if needed to avoid crowding, add the pork pieces and sear, turning as needed, until evenly browned on all sides, about 10 minutes. Transfer to a slow cooker.

Pour off all but 2 tablespoons of the fat from the pan and return to medium-high heat. Add the yellow onion and sear, without stirring, until browned, about 5 minutes. Stir in the garlic, ginger, and 1 cup (240 ml) of the stock and stir to dislodge any browned bits from the pan bottom. Let simmer for 1 minute.

Transfer the contents of the pan to the slow cooker, add the leek, mushrooms, and the remaining 7 cups (1.7 l) broth, and stir to combine. Cover and cook on the low-heat setting for 8 hours. The pork should be very tender and the broth should be fragrant.

Transfer the pork to a cutting board. Using 2 forks, shred the pork into bite-size chunks, removing and discarding any large pieces of fat. Strain the broth through a fine-mesh sieve into a bowl and discard the solids. Let the broth stand for a few minutes, then use a large spoon to skim off and discard any fat from the surface of the broth. Return the pork and broth to the slow cooker and season to taste with soy sauce and sesame and/or chile oil. Cover and cook on the low heat setting for about 30 minutes to warm through.

Cook the ramen noodles according to the package directions. If you want to top each bowl of ramen with an egg, put the eggs into boiling water and boil for 6 minutes. Drain, rinse with cold running water, then remove the shells.

Divide the noodles evenly among individual bowls. Ladle the broth and pork over the noodles, dividing them evenly, then sprinkle with the green onions. If desired, top each bowl with a halved soft-boiled egg and serve.

HOISIN-GINGER PORK LETTUCE WRAPS WITH CASHEW SLAW

Tender braised pork gets a touch of earthy sweetness from the addition of hoisin sauce. Wrap the pork in butter lettuce leaves (as here), spoon into sturdy iceberg lettuce cups, or tuck it into your favorite tortillas to create a no-mess, to-go wrap.

FOR THE PORK

4 lb (1.8 kg) boneless pork shoulder

Kosher salt and freshly ground pepper

1 tablespoon canola oil

½ cup (120 ml) chicken stock

½ cup (120 ml) reduced-sodium soy sauce

½ cup (130 g) hoisin sauce

2 tablespoons Sriracha sauce

4 green onions, thinly sliced

4 cloves garlic, minced

2 tablespoons peeled and shredded fresh ginger

1 tablespoon firmly packed dark brown sugar

FOR THE SLAW

¼ cup (60 ml) rice vinegar

3 tablespoons canola oil

2 teaspoons granulated sugar

Kosher salt

½ head green cabbage

6 green onions, thinly sliced

⅓ cup (20 g) packed chopped fresh cilantro

⅓ cup (40 g) chopped salted roasted cashews

1–2 heads butter lettuce

Hoisin and/or Sriracha sauce, for serving

SERVES 8–10

To make the pork, trim the pork shoulder of excess fat and cut the meat into 4 equal pieces. Season the pork all over with salt and pepper. In a large, heavy frying pan over medium-high heat, warm the oil. Working in batches if needed to avoid crowding, add the pork and cook, turning as needed, until browned on all sides, about 10 minutes. Transfer the pork to a slow cooker.

In a small bowl, combine the stock, soy sauce, hoisin sauce, Sriracha sauce, green onions, garlic, ginger, and sugar and stir to mix well and dissolve the sugar.

Pour the stock mixture evenly over the pork. Cover and cook on the low setting for 6 hours. The pork should be very tender.

Meanwhile, make the slaw. In a large bowl, whisk together the vinegar, oil, sugar, and ½ teaspoon salt until the sugar and salt dissolve. Cut out and remove the core from the cabbage, then thinly slice crosswise. Add the cabbage, green onions, cilantro, and cashews and toss to coat evenly. Cover and refrigerate until ready to use. (The slaw can be made up to 6 hours in advance.)

Transfer the pork to a cutting board. Using 2 forks, pull the pork into shreds, removing and discarding any large bits of fat. Let the cooking liquid stand for a few minutes, then use a large spoon to skim the fat from the surface. Moisten the shredded pork with some of the warm cooking liquid.

To assemble the wraps, gently separate the lettuce leaves, keeping each leaf intact; you'll need 16–18 leaves. Mound some of the pork mixture (¼–⅓ cup/45–55 g, depending on the size of the lettuce leaf) onto each leaf, then top with some slaw (about ¼ cup/25 g). Serve the lettuce wraps right away, with additional hoisin and/or Sriracha sauce on the side for diners to add if they like.

BARBACOA-STYLE PORK WRAP WITH CILANTRO-LIME RICE

In Mexico, barbacoa is typically well-seasoned meat—lamb, beef, goat, pork—slowly roasted over an open fire. In this adaption, that same well-seasoned meat is put into a slow cooker for a go-to weeknight supper. You can swap out the pork for 4 lb (1.8 kg) boneless beef chuck, cut into 2-inch (5-cm) pieces, and cook it the same way.

FOR THE PORK

4 lb (1.8 kg) boneless pork shoulder

Kosher salt and freshly ground pepper

1 tablespoon canola oil

1 yellow onion, finely chopped

6 cloves garlic, minced

¼ cup (60 g) chopped chipotle chiles in adobo sauce, plus 3 tablespoons sauce

2 tablespoons ancho chile powder

1 tablespoon dried oregano

1 tablespoon ground cumin

¼ teaspoon ground cloves

1 cup (240 ml) beef stock or lager-style beer

¼ cup (60 ml) fresh lime juice

¼ cup (60 ml) cider vinegar

1 tablespoon soy sauce

2 bay leaves

Cilantro-Lime Rice (page 173)

12–14 flour tortillas, warmed

Shredded romaine lettuce and chopped red onion or Pickled Onions (page 174), for serving

MAKES 12-14 WRAPS; SERVES 6-14

Trim the pork shoulder of excess fat and cut the meat into 4 equal pieces. Season the pork generously all over with salt and pepper. In a large, heavy frying pan over medium-high heat, warm the oil. Working in batches if needed to avoid crowding, add the pork and cook, turning as needed, until evenly browned on all sides, about 10 minutes. Transfer the pork to a slow cooker.

Return the pan to medium-high heat, add the onion and garlic, and cook, stirring often, until softened, about 6 minutes. Add the chipotle chiles and their sauce, ancho chile powder, oregano, cumin, and cloves and stir to combine. Scrape the mixture into a blender, add the stock, lime juice, vinegar, and soy sauce, and process until smooth.

Pour the chipotle chile mixture over the pork in the slow cooker and tuck in the bay leaves. Cover and cook on the low setting for 6 hours. The pork should be very tender.

Meanwhile, make the cilantro-lime rice. Transfer the pork to a cutting board. Using 2 forks, pull the pork into shreds, removing and discarding any large bits of fat. Let the cooking liquid stand for a few minutes, then use a large spoon to skim the fat from the surface. Return the shredded pork to the warm cooking liquid until ready to use.

Using a slotted spoon, transfer the pork to a bowl. To assemble each wrap, spoon about ¼ cup (40 g) hot rice down the center of a warm tortilla, then top with about ⅓ cup (60 g) pork. Add a small handful of shredded lettuce and some onion. Fold the right and left sides of the tortilla over the filling, overlapping the filling by about 1 inch (2.5 cm). Then, starting at the edge nearest you, roll up the tortilla tightly and place seam side down on a platter. Repeat to make all of the wraps, then serve.

A blend of ancho and chipotle chiles, and plenty of garlic, onion, Mexican herbs, and lime infuse pork with deep flavor.

BRAISED PORK SAUSAGES WITH APPLES, CABBAGE & POTATOES

This German-inspired all-in-one meal cooks slowly and evenly, ensuring the flavors mellow and blend. To expand the menu for a bigger gathering, add warm crusty bread and a green salad. You can trade out the bratwurst for chicken-apple sausages, which will add a sweet accent to the dish.

1 small head green cabbage (about 2¼ lb/1 kg), cored and thinly sliced

2 small yellow onions, thinly sliced

2 tart green apples, such as Granny Smith, peeled, cored, and chopped

1 lb (450 g) Yukon gold potatoes, quartered

2 teaspoons caraway seeds

1 cup (240 ml) chicken broth

1 cup (240 ml) apple cider

⅓ cup (80 ml) cider vinegar

2 tablespoons firmly packed light brown sugar

Kosher salt and freshly ground pepper

1½ lb (680 g) precooked pork sausages, such as bratwurst, sliced

Whole-grain mustard, for serving

SERVES 8–10

In a slow cooker, combine the cabbage, onions, apples, potatoes, caraway seeds, broth, cider, vinegar, brown sugar, 2 teaspoons salt, and 1 teaspoon pepper. Scatter the sausages on top. Cover and cook, stirring once or twice if possible, for 6 hours. The cabbage and potatoes should be very soft.

Using a slotted spoon, spoon the cabbage mixture into warmed bowls and serve warm with mustard.

CIDER-BRAISED PORK ROAST WITH CARAMELIZED ONION–APPLE CONFIT

Here is a foolproof overnight method for making caramelized onions. You can use them in this recipe, or freeze smaller batches for topping burgers, steaks, or pizzas or to dress up a soup. This dish is excellent served over sautéed greens, such as kale, chard, or collard greens, or atop steamed whole grains or Mashed Potatoes (page 173).

FOR THE CARAMELIZED ONIONS

4 large yellow onions, halved and thinly sliced

4 tablespoons (60 g) unsalted butter, melted

Kosher salt

3 Gala apples, peeled, quartered, cored, and each quarter cut lengthwise into 4 wedges

1 cup (240 ml) apple cider

¼ cup (60 ml) calvados (apple brandy) or regular brandy

2 tablespoons whole-grain mustard

1 boneless pork shoulder roast, 4 lb (1.8 kg), tied

Kosher salt and freshly ground pepper

2 tablespoons canola oil

SERVES 8

To make the caramelized onions, the night before serving, put the onions in a slow cooker, add the butter and 1 teaspoon salt, and toss to coat the onions evenly. Cover and cook on the low setting for 10 hours, stirring once in the first few hours if possible. The next morning, stir the onions, re-cover, and cook on the high setting until the onions are golden and most of the liquid has evaporated, 1–2 hours. If the liquid has not evaporated, set the lid ajar for 1–2 hours to evaporate the liquid while the onions continue to cook. (The onions can be caramelized in advance. Let cool to room temperature, then transfer to an airtight container and refrigerate for up to 3 days or freeze for up to 3 months.)

When the onions are ready, add the apples, cider, calvados, and mustard to the onions and stir well.

Season the pork roast generously all over with salt and pepper. In a large, heavy frying pan over medium-high heat, warm the oil. Add the pork and cook, turning as needed, until browned on all sides, about 10 minutes. Transfer the roast to the slow cooker, nestling it into the onion mixture. Cover and cook on the low setting for 8 hours. The pork should be fork-tender.

Transfer the roast to a cutting board, tent with aluminum foil, and let rest for 5 minutes. Let the cooking liquid stand for a few minutes, then use a large spoon to skim the fat from the surface.

Snip and remove the strings from the roast and cut the meat against the grain into slices, discarding any large bits of fat. Arrange the slices on a platter or individual plates. Spoon the onion-apple confit over the pork and serve.

ORANGE-BRAISED PORK CHOPS WITH CRANBERRY COMPOTE

The smell of autumn will fill your house when you make and serve these delicious, sweet, and tangy chops. Don't skip the quick-to-make cranberry relish, which elevates this recipe above the everyday. Plus, the relish can be made well in advance. Accompany the chops with roasted broccoli and mashed sweet potatoes (page 173).

6 bone-in pork loin chops, each about 1½ inches (4 cm) thick

Kosher salt and freshly ground pepper

2 tablespoons olive oil

2 large shallots, halved and thinly sliced

4 cloves garlic, sliced

½ cup (120 ml) dry white wine

½ cup (120 ml) chicken stock

2 tablespoons white wine vinegar

Grated zest of 2 oranges

FOR THE COMPOTE

1¾ cups (175 g) fresh cranberries

½ cup (120 ml) port

½ cup (100 g) sugar

3 tablespoons minced crystallized ginger

SERVES 6

Season the pork chops generously on both sides with salt and pepper. In a large, heavy frying pan over medium-high heat, warm the oil. Working in batches if necessary to avoid crowding, add the chops and sear, turning once, until golden brown on both sides, 8–10 minutes. Transfer the chops to a slow cooker.

Pour off most of the fat in the pan and return the pan to medium-high heat. Add the shallots and garlic and cook, stirring often, until they begin to brown, about 6 minutes. Pour in the wine and stir to dislodge any browned bits from the pan bottom. Stir in the stock, vinegar, orange zest, ½ teaspoon salt, and several grinds of pepper.

Pour the shallot mixture over the pork chops. Cover and cook on the low setting for 6 hours. The chops should be tender.

Meanwhile, make the compote. Fill a large bowl with ice water. In a heavy saucepan, combine the cranberries, port, sugar, and ginger and bring to a boil over high heat, stirring to dissolve the sugar. Reduce the heat to a brisk simmer and cook uncovered, stirring often, until the berries have popped and the juices are syrupy, about 10 minutes. Transfer the compote to a heatproof bowl, set the bowl in the ice bath, and stir the compote occasionally. When the compote is cool, transfer to a serving bowl, cover, and set aside until ready to serve.

Divide the pork chops among individual plates and keep warm. Let the cooking liquid stand for few minutes, then use a large spoon to skim the fat from the surface. Spoon the liquid over the chops, then top the chops with the compote and serve.

MOROCCAN LAMB CHOPS WITH COUSCOUS, PINE NUTS & MINT

Lamb shoulder chops are good candidates for braising because of their relatively high fat content. Look for well-marbled chops for the best results. Couscous flecked with apricots, pine nuts, and mint makes the perfect foundation for the cumin-scented meat.

3 lb (1.4 kg) lamb shoulder chops, trimmed of excess fat

¾ teaspoon ground cumin

Kosher salt and freshly ground pepper

2 tablespoons olive oil

1 large yellow onion, finely chopped

4 cloves garlic, smashed

¼ cup (60 ml) dry red wine

½ cup (120 ml) chicken stock

2 carrots, peeled and chopped

FOR THE COUSCOUS

1⅔ cups (375 ml) chicken stock

1¼ cups (210 g) instant couscous

1 cup (170 g) diced dried apricots

Kosher salt

5 tablespoons (75 ml) extra-virgin olive oil

2 tablespoons sherry vinegar

2 tablespoons pine nuts, lightly toasted, plus more for garnish

2 tablespoons coarsely chopped fresh mint, plus more for garnish

Freshly ground pepper

SERVES 6

Season the lamb chops generously on both sides with the cumin, salt, and pepper. In a large, heavy frying pan over medium-high heat, warm the oil. Working in batches if needed to avoid crowding, add the lamb and sear, turning once, until golden brown on both sides, 8–10 minutes. Transfer the lamb to a plate.

Pour off most of the fat in the pan and return the pan to medium-high heat. Add the onion and cook, stirring often, until lightly golden, about 6 minutes. Add the garlic and cook, stirring, for 1 minute longer. Pour in the wine and stir to dislodge any browned bits from the pan bottom, then stir in the stock.

Transfer the contents of the pan to a slow cooker, add the carrots, and place the lamb and any accumulated juices on top. Cover and cook on the low setting for 8 hours. The meat should be very tender.

Transfer the lamb to a plate and keep warm. Let the braising liquid stand for a few minutes, then, using a large spoon, skim the fat from the surface. Moisten the lamb with some of the liquid and keep the remaining liquid warm.

To make the couscous, in a saucepan over high heat, bring the stock to a boil. Remove from the heat and stir in the couscous, apricots, and ½ teaspoon salt. Cover and let stand for 5 minutes. The liquid should be absorbed. Fluff the couscous with a fork, add the oil, vinegar, pine nuts, mint, and several grinds of pepper, and toss lightly to mix well.

Mound the couscous on a platter, arrange the lamb chops on top, and spoon some of the braising liquid over the lamb. Garnish with more pine nuts and mint and serve.

The mix of dried fruits and nuts in both savory and sweet preparations is a hallmark of Moroccan cooking.

LAMB SHOULDER WITH SALSA VERDE

Loaded with natural flavor, lamb shoulder is an often overlooked cut ideal for braising. You may need to special order it from your butcher, or you can substitute meat from the lamb leg, cut into 3-inch (7.5-cm) pieces. The salsa verde, made with fresh mint and parsley, capers, and Dijon mustard, adds a pleasantly sharp note to this rich dish.

3 lb (1.4 kg) boneless lamb shoulder, trimmed of excess fat and cut into 1¼-inch (3-cm) chunks

Kosher salt and freshly ground pepper

2 tablespoons olive oil

1 large yellow onion, finely chopped

2 fresh thyme sprigs

4 cloves garlic, finely chopped

1 teaspoon dried oregano

⅔ cup (160 ml) dry white wine

1 tablespoon balsamic vinegar

⅔ cup (160 ml) beef or chicken stock

FOR THE SALSA VERDE

2 cloves garlic, chopped

2½ cups (75 g) packed fresh flat-leaf parsley leaves

½ cup (15 g) packed fresh mint leaves

2 tablespoons capers, rinsed

1 tablespoon Dijon mustard

1 tablespoon red wine vinegar

⅔ cup (160 ml) extra-virgin olive oil

SERVES 6

Season the lamb generously all over with salt and pepper. In a large, heavy frying pan over medium-high heat, warm the oil. Working in batches if needed to avoid crowding, add the lamb and sear, turning as needed, until well browned on all sides, about 10 minutes. Using a slotted spoon, transfer the lamb to a slow cooker.

Pour off most of the fat in the pan and return the pan to medium-high heat. Add the onion and thyme and cook, stirring often, until the onion is golden brown, about 6 minutes. Add the garlic and oregano and cook, stirring, for 1 minute longer. Pour in the wine and vinegar and stir to dislodge any browned bits from the pan bottom. Stir in the stock.

Transfer the contents of the pan to the slow cooker. Cover and cook on the low setting for 8 hours. The lamb should be very tender.

About 1 hour before the lamb is ready, make the salsa verde. In a small food processor, combine the garlic, parsley, mint, capers, mustard, and vinegar and pulse until finely chopped. With the processor running, drizzle in the oil in a slow, steady stream and process until smooth. Cover and refrigerate for at least 1 hour or for up to 4 hours before serving.

Using a slotted spoon, divide the lamb among individual plates. Discard the cooking liquid. Drizzle the salsa verde generously over the lamb and serve.

LAMB SHANKS WITH OLIVES & HERBS

Inspired by the flavors of southern France, these meltingly tender lamb shanks are dinner-party worthy. Serve them atop shallow bowls of rich, cheesey polenta (as here), or pair them with roasted fingerling potatoes (page 174) or a mixture of roasted Provençal vegetables, like zucchini, peppers, and tomatoes.

4 lamb shanks, about 1 lb (450 g) each, each tied around the perimeter with kitchen string

Kosher salt and freshly ground pepper

2 tablespoons olive oil

2 carrots, peeled and finely chopped

2 celery stalks, finely chopped

1 red onion, finely chopped

1 teaspoon minced garlic

3 tablespoons all-purpose flour

2 tablespoons tomato paste

½ cup (120 ml) hearty red wine

1 can (14.5 oz/410 g) crushed tomatoes

½ cup (120 ml) fresh orange juice

½ cup (75 g) pitted Kalamata or other black olives

1 tablespoon mild honey

2 teaspoons herbes de Provence

Creamy Parmesan Polenta (page 173)

Chopped fresh flat-leaf parsley, for garnish (optional)

SERVES 4–6

Season the lamb shanks generously all over with salt and pepper. In a large, heavy frying pan over medium-high heat, warm the oil. Add the lamb shanks and sear, turning as needed, until browned on all sides, about 10 minutes. Transfer the shanks to a plate.

Pour off all but 2 tablespoons of the fat in the pan and return the pan to medium-high heat. Add the carrots, celery, onion, and garlic and cook, stirring often, until softened, about 6 minutes. Whisk in the flour and tomato paste and cook, stirring constantly, until the flour is fully incorporated, about 30 seconds. Pour in the wine and simmer, stirring, until well combined, about 2 minutes. Add the tomatoes, orange juice, olives, honey, herbes de Provence, 1 teaspoon salt, and a few grinds of pepper, stir well, bring to a boil, and remove from the heat.

Transfer the contents of the pan to a slow cooker and add the lamb shanks, submerging them in the liquid. Cover and cook on the low setting for 8 hours. The lamb should be very tender.

Transfer the lamb shanks to a platter and keep warm. Let the cooking liquid stand for a few minutes, then use a large spoon to skim the fat from the surface.

About 30 minutes before serving, make the polenta. Divide the polenta among 4 individual bowls. Snip and remove the strings on the lamb shanks, then place the lamb atop the polenta. Spoon the cooking liquid over the shanks, garnish with the parsley (if using), and serve.

LAMB VINDALOO WITH RAITA

You can control the heat in this fiery lamb dish by adjusting the amount of cayenne pepper. The *raita*, a cooling cucumber-yogurt dish, helps temper the fire. If you like, add 1 lb (450 g) peeled and cubed potatoes with the lamb. Serve with warm naan.

3 lb (1.4 kg) boneless leg of lamb or lamb shoulder

¼ cup (60 ml) cider vinegar

3 tablespoons canola oil

Kosher salt

1 large yellow onion, finely chopped

½ cup (120 ml) water

1-inch (2.5-cm) piece fresh ginger, peeled and chopped

4 large cloves garlic, chopped

2 tablespoons firmly packed dark brown sugar

2 teaspoons ground cumin

2 teaspoons ground cinnamon

2 teaspoons ground turmeric

2 teaspoons sweet paprika

2 teaspoons ancho chile powder

½ teaspoon cayenne pepper

½ teaspoon ground cardamom

FOR THE RAITA

½ cup (45 g) shredded cucumber

1 cup (250 g) whole-milk plain yogurt

2 teaspoons fresh lemon juice

½ teaspoon ground cumin

Steamed basmati rice (page 173), for serving

SERVES 6

Cut the lamb meat into 2-inch (5-cm) cubes. In a slow cooker, toss together the lamb cubes, vinegar, 1 tablespoon of the oil, and 2 teaspoons salt.

In a large, heavy frying pan over medium-high heat, warm the remaining 2 tablespoons oil. Add two-thirds of the onion and a pinch of salt and cook, stirring often, until lightly browned, about 6 minutes.

Meanwhile, in a blender, combine the remaining onion, water, ginger, garlic, sugar, cumin, cinnamon, turmeric, paprika, chile powder, cayenne, and cardamom and process until puréed.

Scrape the purée and the cooked onion into the slow cooker and stir to combine all of the ingredients and to coat the lamb evenly. Cover and cook on the low setting for 8 hours. The lamb should be very tender.

Meanwhile, make the raita. Press the cucumber between paper towels to remove the excess moisture. In a bowl, stir together the yogurt, cucumber, lemon juice, and cumin, mixing well. Cover and refrigerate until ready to use.

When the lamb is ready, using a large spoon, skim the fat from the surface of the cooking liquid, then transfer the lamb and its liquid to a serving bowl. Serve the lamb with rice and the raita alongside.

POULTRY

The moist heat
of a slow cooker
contributes tender
consistency to
grains of quinoa.

QUINOA RISOTTO WITH CHICKEN, PESTO, ASPARAGUS & LEMON

Bursting with flavor, this contemporary quinoa dish is a healthy one-pot meal. A splash of lemon juice and a generous measure of basil pesto heighten its overall appeal, while lean chicken adds plenty of protein. Topped just before serving with watercress, asparagus, and herbs, this fresh-tasting main makes a comforting springtime supper.

1½ lb (680 g) skinless, boneless chicken breasts, cut into bite-size pieces

1½ cups (250 g) quinoa, rinsed

4 cloves garlic, minced

4 cups (950 ml) chicken stock

Juice of 1 lemon

Kosher salt and freshly ground pepper

¾ cup (100 g) frozen petite peas

1 tablespoon olive oil

1 lb (450 g) asparagus, tough ends removed and spears cut into 1-inch (2.5-cm) lengths

1 container (7 oz/200 g) fresh basil pesto (about ¾ cup)

½ cup (60 g) freshly grated Parmesan, plus more for serving

2 tablespoons chopped fresh flat-leaf Italian parsley, plus more for serving

2 tablespoons snipped fresh chives, plus more for serving

2 cups (60 g) chopped watercress or baby arugula

SERVES 6

In a slow cooker, combine the chicken, quinoa, garlic, 3 cups (720 ml) of the stock, the lemon juice, 1 teaspoon salt, and ½ teaspoon pepper and stir to mix well. Cover and cook on the low setting for 2½ hours.

Stir in the peas, re-cover, and continue to cook on the low setting for 30 minutes longer. The chicken and quinoa should be tender.

Just before the chicken and quinoa are ready, in a frying pan over medium heat, warm the oil. Add the asparagus, a pinch of salt, and a few tablespoons water, cover the pan, and cook, stirring every so often, until crisp-tender, 2–5 minutes, depending on the thickness of the stalks. Warm the remaining 1 cup (240 ml) stock in the microwave or on the stove top until hot.

When the chicken and quinoa are ready, add the asparagus, hot stock, pesto, Parmesan, parsley, and chives and stir to mix well. Taste and adjust the seasoning with salt, pepper, and lemon juice if needed.

Spoon the risotto into wide, shallow individual bowls and top with the watercress, dividing it evenly. Sprinkle with parsley, chives, and Parmesan and serve.

CHICKEN FAJITAS WITH ONIONS & PEPPERS

Fajitas—traditionally grilled marinated skirt steak—are a mainstay of Tex-Mex cuisine. This variation, using braised chile-rubbed chicken breasts, is significantly easier than the grilled version because it is mostly hands off, yet still tastes great.

1 tablespoon chili powder

1 teaspoon ground cumin

½ teaspoon smoked paprika

Kosher salt

3 lb (1.4 kg) skinless, boneless chicken breast halves

4 tablespoons (60 ml) fresh lime juice

2 tablespoons canola oil

1 yellow onion, thinly sliced

3 bell peppers in assorted colors, seeded and thinly sliced crosswise

1 can (15 oz/425 g) diced tomatoes with juices

2 chipotle chiles in adobo sauce, minced, plus 1 tablespoon sauce

3 cloves garlic, minced

¼ cup (15 g) chopped fresh cilantro

About 20 fajita-size flour tortillas, warmed

Shredded Monterey jack or Cheddar cheese, tomato salsa or pico de gallo, guacamole, sour cream, shredded lettuce, and lime wedges, for serving

MAKES ABOUT 20 FAJITAS; SERVES 8–10

In a large bowl, stir together the chili powder, cumin, paprika, and 2 teaspoons salt. Add the chicken and 2 tablespoons of the lime juice and toss to coat the chicken evenly with the seasonings. Set aside.

In a large, heavy frying pan over high heat, warm the oil. Add the onion, bell peppers, and a sprinkle of salt, stir to combine, and cook, stirring only once or twice, until the edges of the vegetables start to blacken, 5–7 minutes. Remove from the heat and set aside.

In a bowl, stir together the tomatoes and their juices, chipotle chiles and sauce, and garlic, then spoon half of the tomato mixture into the bottom of a slow cooker. Arrange the chicken on top in an even layer, spoon the onion and peppers over the chicken, and finish with the remaining tomato mixture. Cover and cook on the low setting for 4 hours. The chicken should be very tender.

Using a slotted spoon, transfer the chicken to a cutting board. Drain the contents of the slow cooker through a fine-mesh sieve set over a bowl. Return the vegetables to the slow cooker, re-cover, and keep warm on the warm setting. Reserve the strained liquid.

Using 2 forks, shred the chicken into bite-size pieces, removing and discarding any large bits of fat. Return the chicken to the slow cooker, add the remaining 2 tablespoons lime juice, the cilantro, and a few spoonfuls of the cooking liquid to moisten, and stir to mix. Taste and adjust the seasoning with salt.

Set the chicken mixture on the table and arrange the tortillas and bowls with the cheese, salsa, guacamole, sour cream, lettuce, and lime wedges alongside. Invite diners to assemble their own fajitas.

SPICY THAI-STYLE CHICKEN SALAD

Here, chicken perfumed with lemongrass, fish sauce, and garlic is tossed with crisp romaine, cucumber, and carrot, in a dish ideal for a light summer supper. Make the Asian-inspired vinaigrette in advance, then drizzle over the salad just before serving.

3 lb (1.4 kg) skinless, boneless chicken thighs

Kosher salt and freshly ground pepper

1 tablespoon canola oil

1 lemongrass stalk, bulb portion only, tough outer leaves removed, and cut into thick slices

½ large yellow onion, finely chopped

5 cloves garlic, sliced

¼ cup (60 ml) dry white wine

¼ cup (60 ml) fish sauce

½ cup (120 ml) chicken stock

½ small serrano or jalapeño chile, seeded and minced

1 romaine lettuce heart, chopped

4 green onions, thinly sliced

1 carrot, peeled and cut into matchsticks

½ English cucumber, thinly sliced

½ red bell pepper, seeded and thinly sliced

¼ cup (15 g) coarsely chopped fresh cilantro

Lime-Soy Vinaigrette (page 175)

Lime wedges, for serving

SERVES 6

Season the chicken generously all over with salt and pepper and add to a slow cooker.

In a large frying pan over medium-high heat, warm the oil. Add the lemongrass and yellow onion and cook, stirring often, until the onion is golden, about 6 minutes. Add the garlic and cook, stirring, for 1 minute longer. Pour in the wine, fish sauce, and stock. Stir in the chile, ¼ teaspoon salt, and several grinds of pepper. Pour the contents of the pan over the chicken in the slow cooker. Cover and cook on the low setting for 5 hours. The chicken should be very tender.

Using a slotted spoon, transfer the chicken to a plate. Discard the cooking liquid. Using 2 forks, shred the chicken into bite-size pieces. Let cool.

In a bowl, combine the shredded chicken, lettuce, green onions, carrot, cucumber, bell pepper, and half of the cilantro and toss to mix. Drizzle with the vinaigrette and toss to coat evenly. Garnish with the remaining cilantro and serve, accompanied by the lime wedges.

VIETNAMESE-STYLE CHICKEN CURRY

This robust chicken curry is rich with root vegetables, garlic, and ginger. Coconut milk adds a creamy note, and yellow curry powder adds just enough spice and heat. Serve it as is, over rice, or stir in some baby spinach at the end of cooking.

1 tablespoon canola oil

2 shallots, minced

3 cloves garlic, minced

2 lemongrass stalks, trimmed and cut into 1-inch (2.5-cm) pieces

1-inch (2.5-cm) piece fresh ginger, peeled and cut into 4 slices

3 tablespoons Madras-style curry powder

1 tablespoon firmly packed dark brown sugar

1 teaspoon red pepper flakes

Freshly ground pepper

1 cup (8 fl oz/240 ml) chicken broth

1 can (13½ fl oz/400 ml) unsweetened coconut milk

2 tablespoons fish sauce

3 lb (1.4 kg) skinless, bone-in chicken thighs

3 carrots, cut into 1-inch (2.5-cm) chunks

1 sweet potato, about ¼ lb (120 g), peeled and cut into 1-inch (2.5-cm) chunks

3 tablespoons finely shredded fresh basil

Steamed white or brown rice (page 173), for serving (optional)

SERVES 6–8

In a large frying pan over medium-high heat, warm the canola oil. Add the shallots and garlic and cook, stirring, just until fragrant, about 30 seconds. Add the lemongrass, ginger, curry powder, brown sugar, red pepper flakes, and 1 teaspoon pepper and cook, stirring, until the spices are fragrant and well blended with the garlic and shallots, about 30 seconds. Add the broth, coconut milk, and fish sauce and bring to a boil.

Transfer the coconut milk mixture to a slow cooker. Add the chicken thighs, carrots, and sweet potato, pushing them into the mixture. Cover and cook on the low setting for 6 hours. The chicken should be opaque throughout and the vegetables should be tender.

Transfer the chicken, vegetables, and sauce to a warmed platter and garnish with the basil. Serve over steamed rice, if you like.

Flat rice noodles are a classic component of this Vietnamese dish, though the broth-based soup is still delicious without them.

FIVE-SPICE CHICKEN PHO

Pho is an intensely flavored Vietnamese soup that traditionally takes hours of stove-top cooking—and the cook's attention—to create. This simplified version is still bursting with the flavors of star anise, cinnamon, and five-spice powder, but it's a snap to throw together and the slow cooker does most of the work. For a touch of color and fresh flavor, stir in a few handfuls of baby spinach just before serving.

8 cups (1.9 l) chicken stock

1 yellow onion, halved and sliced

3 tablespoons fish sauce

2 cinnamon sticks

4 star anise pods

2-inch (5-cm) piece fresh ginger, peeled and thinly sliced

1 teaspoon five-spice powder

½ teaspoon ground coriander

2 teaspoons sugar

Kosher salt

2½ lb (1.1 kg) skinless, bone-in chicken thighs

¾ lb (340 g) dried flat rice noodles, about ⅛ inch (3 mm) wide

FOR SERVING

Bean sprouts

Thinly sliced jalapeño chiles

Lime wedges

Fresh Thai or sweet basil, cilantro, and/or mint leaves

Sriracha sauce and hoisin sauce

SERVES 6

In a slow cooker, stir together the stock, onion, fish sauce, cinnamon, star anise, ginger, five-spice powder, coriander, sugar, and 1 teaspoon salt. Add the chicken thighs, cover, and cook on the low setting for 6 hours. The chicken should be very tender.

Transfer the chicken to a cutting board. When cool enough to handle, bone the chicken and discard the bones. Using 2 forks, shred the meat into bite-size chunks.

Line a fine-mesh sieve with cheesecloth and strain the cooking liquid through the sieve into a bowl; discard the solids. Return the liquid and the shredded chicken to the slow cooker, cover, and cook on the low setting for 30 minutes to warm through.

While the chicken and cooking liquid are reheating, bring a large pot three-fourths full of water to a boil over high heat. Add the rice noodles and cook until just tender, according to package directions, then drain. Arrange the bean sprouts, jalapeños, lime wedges, and herbs on a platter and set on the table for serving. Set the Sriracha and hoisin sauces alongside the platter.

Divide the noodles evenly among individual bowls and ladle the hot broth and chicken over the noodles. Invite diners to top their soup with the sprouts, chiles, lime juice, herbs, and sauces as desired.

CHICKEN, CORN & POTATO CHOWDER

This recipe has everything you want in a chowder: salty bacon, tender potatoes, sweet corn kernels, and bright herbs, all in a creamy, savory broth. The addition of chicken adds to the heartiness, but you could easily omit it for a simpler soup, or you can replace it with firm white fish, added during the last 20 minutes of cooking.

¼ lb (120 g) applewood-smoked bacon, diced

1 tablespoon unsalted butter

½ yellow onion, finely chopped

1 small red bell pepper, seeded and diced

1 celery stalk, finely chopped

2 lb (900 g) skinless, boneless chicken thighs, cut into 1-inch (2.5-cm) pieces

2 tablespoons all-purpose flour

Kosher salt and freshly ground pepper

1½ lb (680 g) Yukon gold potatoes, peeled and cut into ¾-inch (2-cm) chunks

2 cups (480 ml) chicken stock

½ cup (120 ml) dry white wine

1 bay leaf

2 cups (340 g) fresh or frozen corn kernels

1 cup (240 ml) heavy cream

1 tablespoon finely chopped fresh tarragon, plus more for garnish

1 tablespoon snipped fresh chives, plus more for garnish

SERVES 6–8

In a large, heavy frying pan over medium heat, cook the bacon, stirring often, until crisp, about 5 minutes. Transfer to a paper towel–lined plate and set aside.

Pour off all but 1 tablespoon of the fat in the pan, add the butter, and melt the butter over medium heat. Add the onion, bell pepper, and celery and cook, stirring occasionally, until the vegetables soften, about 6 minutes. Transfer the onion mixture to a slow cooker.

Put the chicken in a bowl, sprinkle with the flour, 2 teaspoons salt, and 1 teaspoon pepper, and toss to coat the chicken evenly. Add the chicken to the slow cooker along with the potatoes, stock, wine, and bay leaf and stir to combine. Cover and cook on the low setting for 5 hours. The chicken should be opaque throughout and the potatoes should be tender.

Add the reserved bacon, the corn kernels, and cream, stir to mix, re-cover, and cook on the low setting until the corn is tender and the chowder is hot, about 1 hour. Stir in the tarragon and chives.

Spoon the chowder into shallow bowls, garnish with tarragon and chives, and serve.

Make this hearty soup dinner party ready with a fresh green salad and a side of Cheddar Biscuits (page 176).

SLOW-COOKED TURKEY & WHITE BEAN CHILI

Simple to prepare yet loaded with complex taste, this turkey and bean chili makes a great winter meal when you want something filling but healthy. Be sure to use dark-meat turkey for the best flavor. And don't skimp on the garnishes—sour cream, green onion, and cilantro—which give this long-cooked dish a fresh finish.

2¼ cups (450 g) dried Great Northern or other small white beans, picked over and rinsed

1 árbol, 1 or 2 serrano, or 1 jalapeño chile, seeded and minced

3 bay leaves

6 cups (1.4 l) chicken stock

1 tablespoon canola oil

1 lb (450 g) ground dark-meat turkey

1 large yellow onion, finely chopped

Kosher salt and freshly ground pepper

5 cloves garlic, minced

2 tablespoons chili powder

1½ tablespoons ground cumin

¼–½ teaspoon cayenne pepper (optional)

Sour cream, for serving

6 green onions, including tender green parts, finely chopped

⅓ cup (20 g) chopped fresh cilantro

SERVES 6

In a large bowl, combine the beans with water to cover by 2 inches (5 cm) and let soak overnight.

Drain the beans and transfer to a slow cooker. Add the chile, bay leaves, and stock. The stock should cover the beans by about 1½ inches (4 cm); add water if needed to reach that level. Cover and cook on the low setting for 6 hours. The beans should be tender.

When the beans are ready, in a large, heavy frying pan over medium heat, warm the oil. Add the turkey and cook, stirring to break it up with a wooden spoon, until the meat is no longer pink, 8–10 minutes. Add the yellow onion, 1 teaspoon salt, and several grinds of pepper and cook, stirring occasionally, until the onion is very soft and lightly golden, about 10 minutes. Add the garlic, chili powder, cumin, and cayenne to taste (if using) and stir together for 2–3 minutes to release their aromas.

Transfer the contents of the pan to the slow cooker and stir to mix with the beans. Raise the heat to the high setting, cover, and cook, stirring one or two times, until slightly thickened, 30–40 minutes.

Season the chili with salt and pepper, then ladle into shallow bowls. Top each serving with a dollop of sour cream, garnish with the green onions and cilantro, and serve.

LEFTOVER TURKEY SOUP WITH FRESH THYME & PASTA

The foundation of this comforting noodle soup is a rich, fully flavored turkey stock that you can use in other recipes as well. If you don't have a turkey carcass, leftover chicken bones—the remains of one or two roasted chickens—will yield an equally delicious result. Dress up the soup with sliced mushrooms or broccoli florets, if you like.

FOR THE STOCK

1 roasted turkey carcass (2–2½ lb/900 g–1.1 kg), large bones broken up

1 yellow onion, chopped, or 1 leek, white and green parts, chopped

1 large carrot, peeled and chopped

2 fresh thyme sprigs

FOR THE SOUP

1 tablespoon olive oil

1 large carrot, peeled and finely chopped

1 large leek, white and pale green parts, trimmed, quartered lengthwise, and thinly sliced crosswise

2 celery stalks, finely chopped

2 teaspoons chopped fresh thyme

Kosher salt and freshly ground pepper

3 cups (500 g) shredded cooked turkey or chicken meat

3 oz (90 g) dried wide egg noodles (about 1½ cups uncooked)

Chopped fresh flat-leaf Italian parsley, for garnish

Lemon wedges, for serving

SERVES 6

To make the stock, break the turkey carcass into pieces small enough to fit in a slow cooker. Put the turkey bones in the slow cooker, then add the onion, carrot, and thyme. Pour in enough water to cover the ingredients by about 1 inch (2.5 cm). Cover and cook on the high setting for 4 hours. Switch to the low setting and continue to cook for 4 hours longer. The stock should be rich tasting and fragrant. (Alternatively, cook the stock on the low setting for 10–12 hours.)

Just before the stock is ready, begin making the soup. In a large frying pan over medium heat, warm the oil. Add the carrot, leek, celery, thyme, 1 teaspoon salt, and ¼ teaspoon pepper and cook, stirring often, until the vegetables are tender, about 10 minutes. Remove from the heat.

When the stock is ready, strain it through a fine-mesh sieve into a large bowl. Discard the solids. You should have about 3 qt (2.8 l) stock. Return the stock to the slow cooker and add the vegetable mixture from the frying pan and the turkey meat. Cover and cook on the high setting for 30 minutes to warm through.

While the soup is heating, bring a large saucepan three-fourths full of salted water to a boil over high heat. Add the noodles and cook until al dente, according to package directions, then drain.

Stir the noodles into the soup, then taste and adjust the seasoning with salt and pepper if needed. Ladle into individual bowls, garnish with parsley, and serve. Pass the lemon wedges at the table for diners to squeeze into their soup.

Garlicky Chicken Thighs
(page 92) with Herbed
Mashed Potatoes
(page 173)

Tarragon Chicken
with Leeks & Carrots
(page 93) with steamed
asparagus

4 WAYS WITH CHICKEN THIGHS

The slow cooker renders chicken thighs perfectly tender and highly versatile. Here are 4 ideas for flavorful chicken dishes that can be served with roasted vegetables, spiralized zucchini or sweet potatoes, brown rice, or herb-mashed potatoes. Use this braising technique as a starting point for your favorite chicken dishes.

Thai Green Curry (page 92)
with spiralized Zucchini
Noodles (page 174)

Fennel, Orange & Olive
Chicken (page 93) with
Steamed Rice (page 173)

GARLICKY CHICKEN THIGHS

Season the chicken with salt and pepper. In a large, heavy frying pan over medium-high heat, warm the oil. Add the chicken, bone side up, and sear until browned on the underside, about 5 minutes. Transfer to a slow cooker.

In the same pan over medium heat, add the onion, garlic cloves, thyme, and bay leaves and cook, stirring often, until the onion and garlic are golden, about 6 minutes. Pour in the wine and vinegar, stir to dislodge any browned bits from the pan bottom, and remove from the heat. Transfer the contents of the pan to the slow cooker, turning the chicken to coat evenly. Cover and cook on the low setting for 6 hours. The chicken should be opaque throughout and tender.

Transfer the chicken thighs to a plate and keep warm. Remove and discard the thyme sprigs and bay leaves. Strain the cooking liquid through a fine-mesh sieve into a small saucepan, reserving the garlic cloves. Let the cooking liquid stand for a few minutes, then, using a large spoon, skim any fat from the surface. Bring to a boil over high heat, and boil until slightly reduced, about 5 minutes.

Divide the chicken evenly among individual plates. Spoon the cooking liquid and garlic cloves over the chicken, garnish with the parsley, and serve.

6 skinless, bone-in chicken thighs (about 3 lb/1.4 kg)

Kosher salt and freshly ground pepper

2 tablespoons olive oil

½ yellow onion, finely chopped

15 cloves garlic, peeled but left whole

2 fresh thyme sprigs

2 bay leaves

⅓ cup (80 ml) dry white wine

1 teaspoon white wine vinegar

Fresh chopped flat-leaf parsley, for garnish

SERVES 6

THAI GREEN CURRY WITH COCONUT MILK

Season the chicken with salt and the zest of 1 lime. Cover and set aside at room temperature for at least 30 minutes or up to overnight in the refrigerator.

In a blender, combine the fish sauce, sugar, curry paste, garlic, yellow onion, the remaining zest of 1 lime, the juice of 2 limes, and half of the cilantro and process until a smooth purée forms.

Pour the onion mixture into a slow cooker, add the coconut milk and stock, and whisk to combine. Add the chicken thighs, submerging them in the liquid. Cover and cook on the low setting for 6 hours. The chicken should be opaque throughout and tender.

Transfer the chicken to a plate. Add the green beans, bell pepper, and green onions to the slow cooker and stir to coat with the sauce. Re-cover and continue to cook on the low setting for 45 minutes. The vegetables should be tender.

Remove and discard the bones from the chicken and break up the meat into large pieces. When the vegetables are ready, return the chicken to the slow cooker, add the remaining cilantro, and stir well. Cook on the low setting until the chicken is warmed through, about 15 minutes. Transfer to a bowl and serve.

6 skinless, bone-in chicken thighs (about 3 lb/1.4 kg)

Kosher salt

Grated zest and juice of 2 limes

3 tablespoons fish sauce

2 tablespoons firmly packed golden brown sugar

2 tablespoons green curry paste

4 cloves garlic, chopped

½ yellow onion, chopped

½ cup (15 g) fresh cilantro leaves

1 can (14 fl oz/425 ml) coconut milk (not light)

1 cup (240 ml) chicken stock

½ lb (225 g) green beans, cut into pieces

1 red bell pepper, seeded and cut into narrow strips

4 green onions, sliced

SERVES 6

TARRAGON CHICKEN WITH LEEKS & CARROTS

Season the chicken with salt and pepper. In a large, heavy frying pan over medium-high heat, warm the oil. Add the chicken, bone side up, and sear until browned on the underside, about 5 minutes. Transfer to a slow cooker.

In the same pan over medium heat, add the leeks, season with salt and pepper, and cook, stirring occasionally, until tender, about 6 minutes. Add the garlic and flour and cook, stirring, for 1 minute longer. Pour in the wine, stirring to dislodge any browned bits from the pan bottom, and cook until thickened, about 1 minute. Stir in 2 tablespoons of the parsley, the tarragon, lemon juice, stock, and carrots and remove from the heat.

Transfer the contents of the pan to the slow cooker, turning the chicken to coat evenly. Cover and cook on the low setting for 6 hours. Stir in the cream and continue to cook for 30 minutes longer. The chicken should be opaque throughout and tender.

Taste and adjust the seasoning with salt and pepper. Divide the chicken evenly among individual plates. Spoon the sauce over the chicken, garnish with the remaining parsley, and serve.

6 skinless, bone-in chicken thighs (about 3 lb/1.4 kg)

Kosher salt and ground pepper

1 tablespoon canola oil

2 large leeks, trimmed and thinly sliced

2 cloves garlic, minced

2 tablespoons all-purpose flour

½ cup (120 ml) dry white wine

3 tablespoons chopped fresh flat-leaf parsley

1 tablespoon chopped fresh tarragon

1 tablespoon lemon juice

1 cup (240 ml) chicken stock

4 carrots, peeled and sliced

½ cup (120 ml) heavy cream

SERVES 6

FENNEL, ORANGE & OLIVE CHICKEN

Season the chicken with salt. In a large, heavy frying pan over medium-high heat, melt the butter with the oil. Add the chicken, bone side up, and sear until browned on the underside, about 5 minutes. Transfer the chicken to a plate.

Grate the zest from the orange and reserve. Halve and juice the orange, then strain the juice through a fine-mesh sieve into a small bowl. You should have about ½ cup (120 ml). Add the grated zest, stock, mustard, and 1 teaspoon salt to the juice and whisk to combine. Transfer the orange mixture to a slow cooker, add the fennel, and toss and stir to mix well. Nestle the chicken pieces, bone side down, in the fennel mixture. Scatter the olives over the chicken. Cover and cook on the low setting for 6 hours. The chicken should be opaque throughout and tender.

Using a slotted spoon, transfer the chicken and fennel to a platter and keep warm. Let the cooking liquid stand for a few minutes, then use a large spoon to skim any fat from the surface.

Divide the chicken and fennel evenly among individual plates. Spoon the cooking liquid over the chicken, garnish with the fennel fronds, and serve.

6 skinless, bone-in chicken thighs (about 3 lb/1.4 kg)

Kosher salt

2 tablespoons unsalted butter

1 tablespoon canola oil

1 large orange

1 cup (240 ml) chicken stock

2 tablespoons whole-grain mustard

2 small fennel bulbs, about 1½ lb (680 g) total weight, trimmed, bulbs cut lengthwise into thin wedges, and small fronds reserved for garnish

⅓ cup (40 g) coarsely chopped pitted Kalamata or Niçoise olives

SERVES 6

This deeply flavored, spiced-up creation offers delicious proof that kale salad is anything but boring.

CHICKEN & BLACK BEAN KALE SALAD

The heart of this healthful salad—chicken and black beans flavored with cumin, chili powder, and lime—also makes a great filling for burritos, soft tacos, or tostadas. Dinosaur kale is called for here, but curly or Red Russian kale can be substituted.

FOR THE CHICKEN AND BLACK BEANS

2 cans (15 oz/425 g each) black beans, drained and rinsed

½ cup (120 ml) chicken stock

¼ cup (60 ml) fresh lime juice

2 tablespoons canola oil

1 tablespoon chili powder

1 teaspoon ground cumin

½ teaspoon smoked paprika

Kosher salt

2 lb (900 g) skinless, boneless chicken thighs

FOR THE VINAIGRETTE

3 tablespoons fresh lime juice

2 tablespoons rice vinegar

¼ cup (15 g) fresh cilantro

⅓ cup (80 ml) extra-virgin olive oil

Pinch of kosher salt

1 large bunch dinosaur kale, tough stems discarded and leaves thinly sliced

2 avocados, halved, pitted, peeled, and thinly sliced

½ lb (225 g) queso fresco cheese, crumbled (optional)

Fresh cilantro leaves, for garnish

Tortilla chips, for serving

SERVES 6–8

To make the chicken and beans, in a slow cooker, combine the beans, stock, lime juice, oil, chili powder, cumin, paprika, and 1½ teaspoons salt and stir to mix well. Add the chicken thighs and, using tongs, turn the chicken to coat evenly with the bean mixture. Cover and cook on the low setting for 5 hours. The chicken should be very tender.

Turn off the slow cooker. Using a slotted spoon, transfer the chicken to a cutting board. Drain the contents of the slow cooker through a fine-mesh sieve set over a bowl and return the beans to the slow cooker. Using 2 forks, shred the chicken into bite-size pieces, discarding any large bits of fat, and return the chicken to the slow cooker. Using a large spoon, skim the fat from the surface of the cooking liquid, then moisten the chicken and beans with a little of the liquid and stir to combine. Taste and adjust the seasoning with salt.

To make the vinaigrette, in a blender, combine the lime juice, vinegar, cilantro, oil, and salt and process until smooth. Pour into a small measuring cup.

Put the kale in a large bowl and add ¼ cup (60 ml) of the vinaigrette. Toss and massage the kale to coat evenly. Arrange the kale on a large serving platter or divide among individual plates. Scatter the chicken and bean mixture over the kale. Top with the avocado, then the cheese (if using), and finally a little cilantro. Drizzle with the remaining vinaigrette and serve. Pass the tortilla chips at the table.

BUFFALO CHICKEN LETTUCE WRAPS

In this updated lettuce-wrapped version of Buffalo chicken wings, you have all of the flavorful goodness of the original and none of the guilt that comes with deep-frying. Here, chicken is gently braised in a beer-based sauce, then shredded, stuffed into crisp lettuce leaves, and topped with salty blue cheese for a fresh-tasting, party-worthy dish.

2 lb (900 g) skinless, boneless chicken thighs, trimmed of excess fat

Kosher salt and freshly ground pepper

1 tablespoon olive oil

½ yellow onion, finely chopped

2 celery stalks, finely chopped

10 cloves garlic, chopped

2 chipotle chiles in adobo sauce, chopped

6 tablespoons (90 g) tomato paste

⅓ cup (80 ml) medium-hot hot-pepper sauce such as Frank's RedHot, plus more for serving

⅓ cup (80 ml) beer

2 tablespoons rice vinegar

1 tablespoon firmly packed golden brown sugar

12 butter or iceberg lettuce leaves

About ¾ cup (100 g) crumbled blue cheese

¼ cup (15 g) chopped fresh flat-leaf Italian parsley

MAKES 12 WRAPS; SERVES 6

Season the chicken all over with salt and pepper and transfer to a slow cooker.

In a frying pan over medium heat, warm the oil. Add the onion, celery, and a pinch of salt and cook, stirring occasionally, until just beginning to brown, about 6 minutes. Add the garlic, chipotle chiles, and tomato paste and cook, stirring, for 1 minute longer. Add the hot-pepper sauce, beer, vinegar, and sugar, and bring to a boil, stirring often. Remove from the heat.

Transfer the contents of the pan to the slow cooker, turning the chicken to coat evenly. Cover and cook on the low setting for 5 hours. The chicken should be very tender.

Using a slotted spoon, transfer the chicken to a plate. Let the sauce stand for a few minutes, then, using a large spoon, skim any fat from the surface. Transfer the sauce to a blender or food processor and process until smooth.

Using 2 forks, shred the chicken into bite-size pieces and transfer to a bowl. Drizzle the chicken with about ½ cup (120 ml) of the sauce and toss gently to coat evenly. (Store any leftover sauce in an airtight container in the refrigerator for up to 1 week or in the freezer for up to 1 month.) Taste and adjust the seasoning with salt and hot-pepper sauce if needed.

To assemble the wraps, arrange the lettuce leaves in a single layer on 1 or 2 large platters and spoon the shredded chicken onto the center of each leaf, dividing it evenly. Top the chicken with a sprinkle of cheese and parsley and serve. Pass additional hot-pepper sauce at the table.

Serve this zesty shredded chicken in lettuce leaves (as here), or use it to top slider buns, crisp tortilla chips, or soft flour tortillas.

MIDDLE EASTERN–STYLE POMEGRANATE CHICKEN

This deeply flavorful dish could not be easier. The secret to the tangy flavor and the rich, dark color of the chicken is pomegranate molasses, an intensely flavored syrup made by cooking down pomegranate juice. Look for it in the international section of well-stocked supermarkets.

½ cup (120 g) dry white wine

⅓ cup (80 ml) pomegranate molasses

⅓ cup (80 ml) fresh lemon juice

3 tablespoons olive oil

3 cloves garlic, minced

1 tablespoon sesame seeds, toasted, plus more for serving

2 teaspoons sumac

1 teaspoon dried oregano

1 teaspoon dried thyme

1 teaspoon dried basil

Kosher salt and freshly ground black pepper

6 skinless, bone-in chicken thighs (about 3 lb/1.4 kg)

SERVES 6

In a slow cooker, whisk together the wine, pomegranate molasses, lemon juice, oil, garlic, sesame seeds, sumac, oregano, thyme, basil, 1 teaspoon salt, and ½ teaspoon pepper, mixing well. Using tongs, add the chicken thighs, turning to coat them with the sauce, then arrange in a single layer. Cover and cook on the low setting for 6 hours. The chicken should be very tender.

Using a slotted spoon, transfer the chicken to a platter and keep warm. Strain the cooking liquid through a fine-mesh sieve into a bowl, let stand for a few minutes, then use a large spoon to skim the fat from the surface.

Pour the cooking juices over the chicken and serve.

CHICKEN WITH LEMON, ALMOND & GREEN OLIVE RELISH

Here, pennywise chicken drumsticks are served with a lemon-olive relish that helps cut the richness of the meat. For the best flavor, look for Picholine, Cerignola, or Lucques olives. Serve the chicken and relish with Steamed Brown Rice (page 173) for soaking up the flavorful juices. Swap the drumsticks for bone-in thighs, if you like.

3 lb (1.4 kg) skinless chicken drumsticks

Kosher salt and freshly ground pepper

4 tablespoons (60 ml) olive oil

½ yellow onion, finely chopped

2 celery stalks, finely chopped

2 fresh thyme sprigs

3 bay leaves

5 cloves garlic, finely chopped

⅓ cup (80 ml) dry white wine

¼ cup (60 ml) chicken stock

1 teaspoon white wine vinegar

FOR THE GREEN OLIVE RELISH

3 small lemons

1¼ cups (175 g) green olives, pitted and finely chopped

⅓ cup (50 g) finely chopped blanched almonds

2 tablespoons finely chopped fresh flat-leaf parsley

SERVES 6

Pat the drumsticks dry, then season all over with salt and pepper. In a large, heavy frying pan over medium-high heat, warm 2 tablespoons of the oil. Working in batches to avoid crowding, add the chicken and sear, turning as needed, until golden brown, about 8 minutes. Transfer the chicken to a slow cooker.

Pour off most of the fat in the pan and return the pan to medium-high heat. Add the onion, celery, thyme, and bay leaves and cook, stirring often, until the vegetables are just beginning to color, about 6 minutes. Add the garlic and cook, stirring, for 1 minute longer. Pour in the wine, stock, and vinegar and stir to dislodge any browned bits from the pan bottom.

Transfer the contents of the pan to the slow cooker, turning the chicken to coat evenly. Cover and cook on the low setting for 4–6 hours. The chicken should be very tender.

While the chicken is cooking, make the relish. Slice 1 lemon crosswise as thinly as possible, preferably with a mandoline or other manual vegetable slicer. Remove the seeds and finely chop the slices, rind and all. In a bowl, combine the chopped lemon, olives, almonds, and parsley. Stir in the remaining 2 tablespoons oil, a scant ¼ teaspoon salt, and a few grinds of pepper.

Transfer the drumsticks to a serving platter and keep warm. Strain the cooking liquid through a fine-mesh sieve into a small saucepan, let stand for a few minutes, and then, using a large spoon, skim any fat from the surface. Reheat over medium heat and keep warm.

Cut the remaining 2 lemons into wedges. Drizzle some of the warm cooking liquid over the chicken, top with the lemon-olive relish, and serve with the lemon wedges on the side.

Finish bowls of this mildly spiced stew with a dollop of sour cream or whole-milk yogurt for an extra touch of richness.

MEXICAN-STYLE CHICKEN SALSA VERDE

Adding sweet corn, fragrant cilantro, and lime juice just 30 minutes before the stew is ready gives this long-simmered dish bright flavor. At the table, garnishes of creamy avocado and crunchy pepitas deliver last-minute texture. This stew is great on its own, but you can extend it for a crowd by serving it over steamed rice (page 173).

3 lb (1.4 kg) skinless, boneless chicken thighs

1 can (28 oz/800 g) whole tomatillos, drained and broken up by hand

2 cans (4 oz/115 g each) fire-roasted diced mild green chiles, drained

1 can (14½ oz/410 g) diced tomatoes with juices

1 yellow onion, finely chopped

4 cloves garlic, minced

1 jalapeño chile, seeded and minced

2 teaspoons dried oregano

2 teaspoons ground cumin

2 cups (475 ml) chicken stock

Kosher salt and freshly ground pepper

1½ cups (250 g) fresh or frozen corn kernels

¼ cup (15 g) chopped fresh cilantro, plus more for garnish

Juice of ½ lime, plus wedges for serving

2 large avocados, halved, pitted, peeled, and sliced, for garnish

About ½ cup (65 g) pepitas (roasted pumpkin seeds), for garnish

SERVES 8

Put the chicken thighs in a slow cooker. Add the tomatillos, green chiles, tomatoes and their juices, onion, garlic, jalapeño, oregano, cumin, stock, 2 teaspoons salt, and ½ teaspoon pepper, and stir to mix well. Cover and cook on the low setting for 5 hours. The chicken should be very tender.

Using a slotted spoon, transfer the chicken to a cutting board. Let the cooking liquid stand for a few minutes, then, using a large spoon, skim the fat from the surface. Using an immersion blender, process the cooking liquid until the solids are roughly puréed. Using 2 forks, shred the chicken, discarding any large bits of fat.

Return the chicken to the slow cooker, add the corn, cilantro, and lime juice, and stir to combine. Cover and cook on the low setting until the corn is tender and the chicken is heated through, about 30 minutes. Taste and adjust the seasoning with salt, pepper, and lime juice if needed.

Ladle into individual bowls and garnish with the avocado, pepitas, and cilantro. Finish with a squeeze of lime juice and serve.

INDIAN-SPICED CHICKEN WITH TOMATOES & CREAM

This simplified slow cooker rendition of chicken tikka masala is deliciously family-friendly. Serve it over steamed rice as suggested, or stir in some sautéed greens or petite peas and pass toasted whole-wheat naan on the side for a complete meal.

1 tablespoon ground cumin

1 tablespoon sweet paprika

2 teaspoons ground coriander

2 teaspoons garam masala

Kosher salt

3 lb (1.4 kg) skinless, boneless chicken breast halves

1 tablespoon peeled and grated fresh ginger

4 cloves garlic, minced

Juice of ½ lemon

2 tablespoons unsalted butter or ghee

1 small yellow onion, finely chopped

1 can (15 oz/425 g) diced tomatoes, drained

¼ cup (60 g) tomato paste

2–4 teaspoons sugar

1 cup (240 ml) heavy cream

¼ cup (15 g) chopped fresh cilantro, plus more for garnish

Steamed basmati rice (page 173), for serving

SERVES 6

In a small bowl, stir together the cumin, paprika, coriander, garam masala, and 2 teaspoons salt, mixing well. Put the chicken in a large lock-top plastic bag, add the ginger, garlic, lemon juice, and 3 tablespoons of the spice mixture, and seal the bag closed. Massage the chicken in the bag to coat it evenly. Cover the remaining spice mixture and set aside, then refrigerate the chicken for at least 2 hours or preferably overnight.

About 10 minutes before you are ready to cook, in a frying pan over medium heat, melt the butter. Add the onion and cook, stirring occasionally, until it softens, about 6 minutes. Add the reserved spice mixture and cook, stirring, until fragrant, about 1 minute. Add the diced tomatoes and tomato paste and stir well. Taste and add the sugar as needed if the tomato mixture is too acidic. Bring to a simmer.

Put the chicken in a slow cooker, pour in the tomato mixture, and, using tongs, turn the chicken to coat evenly with the sauce. Cover and cook on the low setting for 4 hours. The chicken should be opaque throughout and tender.

Using a slotted spoon, transfer the chicken to a cutting board. Let the sauce stand for a few minutes, then use a large spoon to skim the fat from the surface. Pour the cream into the sauce and stir to mix. Then, using an immersion blender, process the sauce until smooth. Leave the sauce uncovered on the low setting while you prepare the chicken. (Or, if you prefer the sauce a bit thicker, transfer it to a saucepan and simmer over medium-low heat until slightly thickened, about 10 minutes, then return the sauce to the slow cooker.)

Using 2 forks, shred the chicken into large bite-size pieces, discarding any large bits of fat. Return the chicken to the slow cooker, add the cilantro, stir well, cover, and cook on the low setting until the chicken is warmed through, 15–30 minutes. Taste and adjust the seasoning with salt and/or lemon juice if needed.

Transfer the chicken and sauce to a serving bowl or individual plates, garnish with cilantro, and serve, accompanied with rice.

CHICKEN, LEEK & MUSHROOM STEW WITH CHEDDAR BISCUITS

This savory, creamy chicken-and-vegetable stew is terrific served topped with hot, baked cheese biscuits. You can also easily turn this recipe into a potpie by omitting the biscuits and following the method for Beef & Mushroom Potpie (page 43).

3 tablespoons unsalted butter

1 small yellow onion, finely chopped

1 large leek, white and pale green parts, trimmed, quartered lengthwise, and sliced crosswise

2 carrots, peeled and diced

2 celery stalks, diced

1 teaspoon dried thyme

1 teaspoon dried oregano

Kosher salt and freshly ground pepper

½ cup (60 g) all-purpose flour

½ cup (120 ml) dry white wine

1¾ cups (425 ml) chicken stock

1 cup (240 ml) half-and-half

2 lb (900 g) boneless, skinless chicken thighs

½ lb (225 g) cremini mushrooms, brushed clean, stem ends trimmed, and thickly sliced

Cheddar Biscuits (page 176)

SERVES 6

In a frying pan over medium heat, melt the butter. Add the onion, leek, carrots, celery, thyme, oregano, and 1 teaspoon salt and cook, stirring, until the vegetables begin to soften, about 6 minutes. Sprinkle the flour over the vegetables and stir to coat evenly. Slowly add the wine, then the stock, and finally the half-and-half while stirring constantly. Continue to cook, stirring, until the mixture thickens, about 1 minute. Remove from the heat.

Transfer the contents of the pan to a slow cooker. Add the chicken, mushrooms, and 1 teaspoon salt and stir to mix well. Cover and cook on the low setting for 4 hours, stirring once or twice during cooking if possible. The chicken should be very tender.

About 30 minutes before the stew is ready, make the biscuits. To serve, spoon the chicken stew into shallow bowls and top each bowl with 2 warm biscuits, or split the biscuits and spoon the stew over the top.

SEAFOOD

A flavorful fish stock makes
all the difference in this
updated classic. Prepare
your own (page 171) or find
it in the freezer section
of a well-stocked market.

FRENCH FISH STEW WITH FINGERLINGS, AIOLI & CROSTINI

You can prepare this stew from the French fishing port of Marseilles in the traditional way, stirring the aioli into the strained liquid and then simmering gently to thicken, or you can top each serving with a dollop of aioli for diners to swirl into their bowls.

3 tablespoons olive oil

1 lb (450 g) fingerling or Yukon gold potatoes, cut into ½-inch (12-mm) pieces

1 small fennel bulb, trimmed, cored, and thinly sliced crosswise

1 leek, white and pale green parts, halved lengthwise and thinly sliced crosswise

1 large, ripe tomato, halved, seeded, and finely chopped

½ yellow onion, finely chopped

1 carrot, peeled and finely diced

Kosher salt and freshly ground pepper

2 cups (480 ml) fish stock

1 cup (240 ml) dry white wine

2 cloves garlic, minced, plus 1 large clove

1 large bay leaf

Aioli (page 171)

Crostini (page 176)

2 lb (900 g) skinned firm, thick white fish fillets such as halibut, mahimahi, or cod, cut into 1-inch (2.5-cm) pieces

2 tablespoons chopped fresh flat-leaf parsley, for garnish

SERVES 6

In a large, heavy frying pan over medium heat, warm the oil. Add the potatoes, fennel, leek, tomato, onion, carrot, and 1 teaspoon salt and cook, stirring occasionally, until the vegetables soften, about 5 minutes. Add the stock, wine, garlic, and bay leaf and stir to mix. Transfer the contents of the pan to a slow cooker, cover, and cook on the low setting for 2 hours. The vegetables should be tender.

While the stew cooks, make the aioli and crostini; set aside.

Add the fish to the slow cooker and stir to coat with the cooking liquid. Re-cover and cook on the low setting until the fish is opaque throughout, about 10 minutes.

Using a slotted spoon, transfer the fish and vegetables to a shallow serving bowl and cover to keep warm. Pour the liquid through a fine-mesh sieve into a saucepan. Add any solids in the sieve to the serving bowl, discarding the bay leaf. Whisk ½ cup (60 ml) of the aioli into the strained liquid, then bring to a simmer over medium heat on the stove top and cook, whisking constantly, until warmed through, about 5 minutes.

Pour the hot liquid over the fish mixture, garnish with the parsley, and serve, accompanied with the crostini. The remaining aioli can be served for spreading on the crostini, or it can be stored in an airtight container in the refrigerator for up to 1 week.

BASQUE-STYLE COD WITH PIPERADE, OLIVES & PARSLEY

Piperade, a Basque dish of sweet peppers, tomatoes, plenty of garlic, and medium-hot Espelette chile, makes a wonderful topping for braised fish. In this variation, the addition of salty-tangy green olives and a garlicky parsley garnish heightens the overall flavor of the dish. Chop the olives and mix them in with the parsley, if you like. Roasted potatoes (page 174) are an ideal accompaniment.

3 tablespoons tomato paste

5 tablespoons olive oil

¾ teaspoon piment d'Espelette or regular (unsmoked) paprika

Salt and freshly ground pepper

15 cloves garlic, smashed, plus 2 garlic cloves, finely chopped

1 large yellow onion, halved and thinly sliced

1 green, 1 yellow, and 2 red bell peppers, seeded and cut lengthwise into thin strips

1½ lb (680 g) cod fillets

2 tablespoons coarsely chopped fresh flat-leaf parsley

1 tablespoon sherry vinegar

½ cup (70 g) pitted picholine olives or Spanish green olives

SERVES 6

In a slow cooker, whisk together the tomato paste, 3 tablespoons of the oil, piment d'Espelette, 1 teaspoon salt, and several grinds of pepper. Add the smashed garlic cloves, onion, and bell peppers and mix well. Cover and cook on the low setting for 4 hours, stirring two or three times if possible. Stir the peppers, add the fish, re-cover and continue cooking for 30 minutes. The fish should be firm yet very tender and the peppers should be tender.

Meanwhile, in a small bowl, stir together the parsley, finely chopped garlic, remaining 2 tablespoons oil, and the vinegar. Set aside.

Using a slotted spoon, transfer the fish and peppers to a platter or divide among individual plates. Drizzle the mixture over the peppers and fish, garnish with the whole olives, and serve.

OLIVE OIL–BRAISED TUNA WITH TAPENADE

In this French-inspired recipe, a hefty measure of extra-virgin olive oil keeps the tuna moist and tender as it slowly braises. An orange-scented tapenade adds a welcome briny counterpoint to the rich fish. Here, we've served the tuna warm on a bed of fresh greens, but you can also let it cool to room temperature and add it to a salad.

¼ cup (60 ml) fish or vegetable stock

5 tablespoons (75 ml) extra-virgin olive oil, plus more for drizzling

¼ cup (60 ml) dry white wine

½ yellow onion, finely chopped

3 bay leaves

Kosher salt and freshly ground pepper

4 skinless tuna fillets or steaks, about 6 oz (170 g) each

1 cup (140 g) pitted mild green olives such as Picholine or Lucques

1 cup (140 g) pitted mild black olives such as Niçoise

2 cloves garlic, chopped

1 teaspoon red or white wine vinegar

Grated zest of 1 orange

4 cups (120 g) baby spinach

SERVES 4

In a slow cooker, stir together the stock, 4 tablespoons (60 ml) of the oil, the wine, onion, bay leaves, ½ teaspoon salt, and several grinds of pepper. Cover and cook on the low setting for 30 minutes to blend the flavors.

Add the tuna, re-cover, and cook on the low setting for 15–20 minutes. The tuna should be firm. After about 15 minutes, it will still be slightly pink at the center; after 20 minutes, it will be opaque throughout.

Meanwhile, make the tapenade. In a food processor, combine the green and black olives, garlic, the remaining 1 tablespoon oil, the vinegar, and orange zest. Pulse to form a chunky tapenade. (You will not need all of the tapenade for this recipe. Transfer the leftover tapenade to an airtight container and refrigerate for up to 1 week; use the tapenade as a sandwich spread, or serve it with cheese and the Crostini on page 176.)

Put the spinach in a bowl, drizzle with a little oil, season with salt and pepper, and toss to coat evenly. Divide the spinach evenly among individual plates. Using a slotted spatula, transfer the tuna to the plates, arranging it on top of the spinach. Discard the cooking liquid. Top each tuna portion with a spoonful of the tapenade and serve.

AHI TUNA WITH HERBED WHITE BEANS

This contemporary take on a classic combination pairs tender braised tuna and creamy beans with aromatic thyme, a tangy vinaigrette, and a final sprinkling of lemon zest. Perfect for a midday meal, this dish is delicious served atop a pile of salad greens or on thick slices of whole-grain toast.

4 tablespoons (120 ml) olive oil

½ small yellow onion, finely chopped

6 cloves garlic, finely chopped

3 fresh thyme sprigs

1 can (15 oz/425 g) diced tomatoes, drained

½ cup (120 ml) vegetable stock

½ cup (120 ml) dry white wine

Kosher salt and freshly ground pepper

¾ lb (340 g) skinless yellowfin (ahi) tuna fillet

1 can (15 oz/425 g) white beans, drained and rinsed

1 tablespoon red wine vinegar

¼ red onion, thinly sliced

2 tablespoons chopped fresh flat-leaf parsley

Grated zest of 1 lemon

SERVES 4

In a frying pan over medium heat, warm 1 tablespoon of the oil. Add the onion, garlic, and thyme and cook, stirring, until softened, about 6 minutes. Add the tomatoes, stock, wine, ½ teaspoon salt, and several grinds of pepper. Bring to a boil, then remove from the heat and transfer to a slow cooker. Cover and cook on the low setting for 1 hour to blend the flavors.

Add the tuna, re-cover, and cook for 15–20 minutes. The tuna should be firm. After about 15 minutes, it will still be slightly pink at the center; after 20 minutes, it will be opaque throughout.

Meanwhile, in a bowl, combine the beans, the remaining 3 tablespoons oil, the vinegar, red onion, half each of the parsley and lemon zest, ¼ teaspoon salt, and several grinds of pepper. Stir well, then taste and adjust the seasoning with salt and pepper if needed.

Using a slotted spatula, transfer the tuna and vegetables to a plate. Discard the cooking liquid. Using 2 forks, pull the tuna apart into large flakes.

Divide the bean mixture evenly among individual plates. Top the beans with the flaked tuna and vegetables, garnish with the remaining parsley and lemon zest, and serve.

Sea bass is a dense, firm white fish that adapts well to slow cooking. Halibut, mahi mahi, and cod are also good options.

COCONUT SEA BASS CURRY

Inspired by the Kerala-style fish curries of India's southwest coast, this exquisite dish draws on tart tamarind, spicy ginger, chile, mustard seeds, and spices for its complex flavor and coconut milk for its irresistible creaminess. Serve the curry over sautéed greens with naan alongside, or stay classic with a side of basmati rice (page 173).

1 tablespoon canola oil

1 small or ½ large yellow onion, finely chopped

Kosher salt

2 tomatoes, halved, seeded, and finely chopped

3 tablespoons tamarind chutney

1 heaping tablespoon peeled and grated fresh ginger

1 teaspoon ground coriander

1 teaspoon ancho or other medium-hot chile powder

1 teaspoon yellow mustard seeds

½ teaspoon ground turmeric

1 can (14 fl oz/425 ml) coconut milk (not light), shaken well before opening

2 lb (900 g) skinless thick sea bass, halibut, or cod fillet, cut into 1½-inch (4-cm) pieces

Fresh cilantro leaves, for garnish

SERVES 6

In a frying pan over medium heat, warm the oil. Add the onion and a pinch of salt and cook, stirring occasionally, until lightly golden, about 6 minutes. Add the tomatoes, chutney, ginger, coriander, chile powder, mustard seeds, turmeric, and 1 teaspoon salt and cook, stirring, until the tomatoes start to break down and the spices are fragrant, about 5 minutes.

Transfer the tomato mixture to a slow cooker, add the coconut milk, and stir to mix well. Cover and cook on the low setting for 1 hour to blend the flavors.

Add the fish and stir to coat the fish evenly. Cover and cook on the low setting for 30 minutes. The fish should be opaque throughout.

Divide the curry among individual bowls, garnish with cilantro, and serve.

MISO-POACHED SALMON WITH SESAME SOBA NOODLES

Salmon poached in fragrant miso, ginger, and garlic is great served atop a bed of steamed rice, zucchini noodles, or sautéed spinach tossed with toasted sesame oil, but even better over sesame-kissed soba with plenty of green onions. Look for good-quality soba—thin, brownish noodles made from buckwheat, usually with wheat flour mixed in—at Asian food shops or well-stocked supermarkets.

1½ cups (350 ml) vegetable or fish stock or water

⅓ cup (70 g) white (shiro) miso

1 tablespoon peeled and shredded fresh ginger

2 cloves garlic, minced

2–2½ lb (900–950 g) skin-on salmon fillet, cut into 4 or 6 equal pieces

FOR THE SOBA

1 lb (450 g) dried soba

1–2 tablespoons reduced-sodium soy sauce, or to taste

2 teaspoons toasted sesame oil

2 teaspoons canola oil

3–4 green onions, including tender green parts, thinly sliced

1 tablespoon sesame seeds, toasted

1–2 green onions, including tender green parts, thinly sliced

1–2 tablespoons sesame seeds, toasted

SERVES 4–6

In a slow cooker, whisk together the stock, miso, ginger, and garlic. Cover and cook on the low setting for 2 hours. The mixture should be hot and fragrant.

Using tongs, add the salmon fillets and turn to coat them evenly with the liquid, then leave them, skin side down, in a single layer. Cover and cook on the low setting until just barely opaque at the center and firm, about 30 minutes.

While the salmon is cooking, prepare the soba. Bring a large pot three-fourths full of salted water to a boil over high heat. Add the soba and cook, stirring frequently to prevent the noodles from sticking together, until just tender, according to package directions. Drain and transfer to a large bowl. Add the soy sauce, sesame oil, canola oil, green onions, and the sesame seeds and toss to mix evenly. Transfer the noodles to a platter.

Using a slotted spatula, transfer the salmon to a cutting board; peel off and discard the skin. Arrange the salmon on the soba noodles. Strain the cooking liquid through a fine-mesh sieve into a small bowl and set alongside the platter. Garnish the salmon and noodles with the green onions and the sesame seeds and serve.

Toss the soba in soy sauce and sesame oil when still warm— it's the best way to cloak the noodles with their flavors.

BRAISED SALMON WITH TAMARI, LEMON & GINGER

In this easy meal, a mixture of lemon juice and zest, fresh ginger, soy sauce, and brown sugar creates a salmon dish with big flavors. Serve with a quick sauté of sugar snap peas or asparagus and plenty of steamed rice for soaking up the delicious sauce.

¼ cup (60 ml) tamari or reduced-sodium soy sauce

Grated zest of 1 large lemon

Juice of 2 large lemons

1 heaping tablespoon peeled and grated fresh ginger

2 tablespoons firmly packed golden brown sugar

6 skin-on salmon fillets, about 6 oz (170 g) each

SERVES 6

In a slow cooker, combine the tamari, lemon zest and juice, ginger, and sugar and stir until the sugar dissolves. Using tongs, add the salmon fillets and turn to coat them evenly with the sauce, then leave them, skin side down, in a single layer. Let stand at room temperature for 15 minutes.

Cover the slow cooker and cook on the low setting for 30 minutes. The fish should be opaque throughout.

Using a slotted spatula, transfer the salmon fillets to a platter. Strain the cooking liquid through a fine-mesh sieve into a small bowl. Set the bowl alongside the platter and serve.

SLOW-SIMMERED SALMON WITH SPRING VEGETABLES

The rich flavor of salmon pairs nicely with such springtime favorites as asparagus, peas, and leeks. To keep the vegetables fresh tasting and tender-crisp, they are cooked quickly on the stove top and seasoned simply with lemon juice, salt, and pepper.

1 cup (240 ml) dry white wine

½ cup (120 ml) water

½ cup (120 ml) vegetable stock

½ small yellow onion, sliced

3 fresh tarragon sprigs

Kosher salt and freshly ground pepper

4 skinless salmon fillets, about 6 oz (170 g) each

1 bunch asparagus, about 1 lb (450 g), tough ends removed and spears cut into 2-inch (5-cm) lengths

1 tablespoon unsalted butter

1 tablespoon olive oil

2 leeks, white and pale green parts, cut into matchsticks

2 cups (285 g) fresh or thawed frozen English peas

Grated zest and juice of ½ lemon

Snipped fresh chives, for garnish

SERVES 4

In a slow cooker, stir together the wine, water, stock, onion, tarragon, ½ teaspoon salt, and several grinds of pepper. Cover and cook on the low setting for 1 hour to blend the flavors.

Add the salmon fillets in a single layer (they can overlap), re-cover, and cook on the low setting for 30 minutes. The fish should be opaque throughout.

About 15 minutes before the fish is ready, bring a saucepan three-fourths full of salted water to a boil over high heat. Add the asparagus and cook until tender-crisp, 2–5 minutes. Drain and run under cold running water until cool. Spread on a kitchen towel to dry.

In a large frying pan over medium heat, melt the butter with the oil. Add the leeks and cook, stirring occasionally, for 2 minutes. Add the peas and cook, stirring, for 2 minutes, then add the asparagus and cook, stirring, until heated through, 1–2 minutes longer. Stir in the lemon juice, season lightly with salt and pepper, and remove from the heat.

Using a slotted spatula, transfer the salmon fillets to individual plates. Discard the cooking liquid. Arrange the vegetables alongside the salmon, dividing them evenly. Scatter the lemon zest and chives over the fish and serve.

Steamed rice is the classic partner to these spicy-sweet fillets, but mashed sweet potatoes (page 173) or Sautéed Greens (page 174) are also tasty sides.

VIETNAMESE-STYLE CARAMELIZED FISH WITH GINGER

In Vietnam, this dish is traditionally made in a clay pot with catfish. In this updated version, sugar is caramelized on the stove top, mixed with umami-rich fish sauce, coconut water, ginger, onion, and garlic, then combined with meaty white fish in a slow cooker. Choose a fish fillet no less than 1 inch (2.5 cm) thick for the best result. The size of the fillet will determine the cooking time, so check the fish regularly to avoid overcooking.

½ cup (100 g) sugar

2 tablespoons water

1 tablespoon fresh lemon juice

½ cup (120 ml) coconut water

¼ cup (60 ml) fish sauce

2 tablespoons canola oil

½ yellow onion, halved and thinly sliced

3 cloves garlic, minced

1-inch (2.5-cm) piece fresh ginger, peeled and shredded

2 fresh red Thai chiles, seeded and thinly sliced crosswise

3 green onions, including tender green parts, sliced

2 lb (900 g) skinless firm, mild, white fish fillet such as halibut or cod, cut into 6 equal pieces

Kosher salt and freshly ground pepper

Steamed jasmine rice (page 173), for serving

SERVES 6

In a heavy saucepan over medium-high heat, stir together the sugar, water, and lemon juice. Cook, swirling the pan occasionally to ensure even cooking (do not stir), until the sugar melts, comes to a boil, and turns a deep caramel brown, about 5 minutes. As the caramel cooks, use a brush dipped in cold water to wash down any sugar crystals that form on the pan sides and watch carefully to prevent burning. Remove from the heat, then carefully whisk in the coconut water and fish sauce until well combined. Transfer the contents of the pan to a slow cooker.

Return the saucepan to medium-high heat and warm the oil. Add the yellow onion, garlic, ginger, and chiles and cook, stirring often, until just starting to soften, about 5 minutes.

Transfer the onion mixture to the slow cooker, add the green onions, and stir to combine. Cover and cook on the low setting for 2 hours to blend the flavors.

Season the fish on both sides with salt and pepper. Using tongs, add the fish to the slow cooker and turn to coat evenly with the sauce. Re-cover and cook on the low setting until the fish is firm and opaque throughout, about 25 minutes.

Spoon the rice onto individual plates. Using a slotted spatula, place the fish atop the rice, then spoon the sauce over the fish and serve.

BOUILLABAISSE WITH FENNEL & ORANGE ZEST

Preparing a traditional bouillabaisse can take hours of hands-on time, but the slow cooker simplifies this popular Provençal fish stew, freeing up the cook's time in the process. This recipe calls only for fish, but if you like clams, mussels, and shrimp, add a few handfuls of each during the last 15 minutes of cooking.

2 tablespoons olive oil

10 cloves garlic, thinly sliced

1 tablespoon fennel seeds

3 bay leaves

¼ cup (60 g) tomato paste

Kosher salt and freshly ground pepper

⅓ cup (80 ml) dry white wine

1 large fennel bulb

1 can (15 oz/425 g) crushed tomatoes with juices

5 cups (40 fl oz/1.25 l) fish or vegetable stock

2 lb (900 g) skinless cod or monkfish fillets, cut into 2-inch (5-cm) chunks

Grated zest of 1 orange

2 tablespoons chopped fresh chervil (optional)

Crostini (page 176), for serving

SERVES 4–6

In a large, heavy frying pan over low heat, warm the oil. Add the garlic, fennel seeds, and bay leaves and cook gently, stirring occasionally, until the garlic is fragrant and tender, about 10 minutes. Do not let the garlic brown. Stir in the tomato paste and 1½ teaspoons salt and cook, stirring, for 2 minutes. Pour in the wine and stir to combine. Transfer the contents of the pan to a slow cooker.

Cut off the stems and feathery tops and any bruised outer stalks from the fennel bulb. Discard the stems and bruised stalks. Coarsely chop the feathery tops to yield 2 tablespoons and set aside. Cut the bulb lengthwise into wedges and trim away the core, leaving a little core intact to hold each wedge together. Add the fennel wedges, tomatoes and their juices, and stock to the slow cooker, stir to combine, cover, and cook on the low setting for 3 hours.

Add the fish, stir gently, re-cover, and cook for 30 minutes more. The fish should be opaque throughout.

Using a slotted spoon, transfer the fish and fennel wedges to a large plate. Remove and discard the bay leaves from the cooking liquid. Using an immersion blender, purée what remains in the slow cooker until smooth. (Alternatively, for a chunkier soup, transfer half of the mixture to a stand blender, process until smooth, then return the purée to the slow cooker and stir to combine.)

Ladle the tomato broth from the slow cooker into shallow bowls and divide the fish and fennel wedges evenly among the bowls. Garnish each serving with a little orange zest, the chopped fennel tops, and the chervil, if using, and serve, accompanied by the crostini.

BRAISED SALMON WITH CUCUMBER-YOGURT SALAD

The slow cooker brings out the succulent texture of salmon, a fish rich in good-for-you omega-3 fatty acids. Here, simply braised salmon is paired with an herb-laced salad of cucumber and yogurt, but it can also be stirred into scrambled eggs, spread atop an avocado-smeared bagel, tossed with pasta, or used in place of tuna in a Niçoise salad.

1 cup (240 ml) dry white wine

½ cup (120 ml) water

½ cup (120 ml) vegetable stock

½ small yellow onion, sliced

3 fresh dill sprigs

½ teaspoon kosher salt

Freshly ground pepper

6 skinless salmon fillets, about 5 oz (140 g) each

FOR THE SALAD

1 cup (250 g) plain yogurt

1 tablespoon mayonnaise

1 shallot, minced

3 tablespoons coarsely chopped fresh dill

3 tablespoons coarsely chopped fresh flat-leaf parsley

¼ teaspoon ground cumin

1 English cucumber, halved lengthwise and thinly sliced crosswise

Kosher salt and freshly ground pepper

1 tablespoon coarsely chopped fresh dill

1 tablespoon coarsely chopped fresh flat-leaf parsley

SERVES 6

In a slow cooker, stir together the wine, water, stock, onion, dill, salt, and several grinds of pepper. Cover and cook on the low setting for 1 hour to blend the flavors.

Add the salmon fillets in a single layer (they can overlap), re-cover, and cook on the low setting for 30 minutes. The fish should be opaque throughout.

Meanwhile, make the salad. In a bowl, whisk together the yogurt, mayonnaise, shallot, dill, parsley, and cumin. Add the cucumber and stir to mix well. Season with salt and pepper.

Using a slotted spatula, transfer the salmon fillets to individual plates. Discard the cooking liquid. Spoon an equal amount of the salad over each salmon fillet, then garnish with the dill and parsley and serve.

SHRIMP & CHICKEN GUMBO

This easy, flavorful gumbo promises to become a family favorite. If you cannot imagine gumbo without okra, add 2 cups (200 g) sliced fresh okra 1 hour before the gumbo has finished cooking and omit the filé powder (fragrant, earthy ground sassafras leaves, which, like okra, help thicken the gumbo). To make the gumbo in advance, prepare it through shredding the chicken and returning it to the pot, then wait to add the filé powder and shrimp until just before you are ready to serve.

2 lb (900 g) skinless, bone-in chicken thighs

Kosher salt and freshly ground pepper

3 tablespoons unsalted butter

3 tablespoons canola oil

½ cup (60 g) all-purpose flour

1 yellow onion, finely chopped

1 small green bell pepper, seeded and diced

1 small red bell pepper, seeded and diced

1 large celery stalk, diced

2 tablespoons tomato paste

1 tablespoon Cajun seasoning

3 cloves garlic, minced

3 cups (700 ml) chicken stock

1 can (14½ oz/410 g) diced tomatoes with juices

2 teaspoons filé powder

1 lb (450 g) medium shrimp, peeled and deveined, with tails intact

Steamed White Rice (page 173), for serving

SERVES 8–10

Season the chicken generously all over with salt and pepper. Put the chicken in a slow cooker.

In a large, heavy frying pan over medium heat, melt the butter with the oil. Sprinkle the flour over the butter and oil and whisk to combine. Cook, stirring constantly, until the mixture thickens and turns a rich caramel brown, about 10 minutes. Add the onion, bell peppers, celery, and a pinch of salt and cook, stirring constantly, until the vegetables have softened, about 7 minutes. Add the tomato paste, Cajun seasoning, and garlic and stir until well combined. Slowly add the stock while stirring constantly, then add the tomatoes and their juices and stir to mix well.

Pour the tomato mixture over the chicken. Cover and cook on the low setting for 6 hours. The chicken should be tender.

Using a slotted spoon, transfer the chicken to a cutting board. Let the cooking liquid stand for a couple of minutes, then, using a large spoon, skim the fat from the surface. Cover the slow cooker and keep on the warm setting while you prepare the chicken.

When the chicken is cool enough to handle, bone it and discard the bones and any large bits of fat. Using 2 forks, pull the meat into bite-size pieces. Return the chicken to the slow cooker, cover, and cook on the low setting for 30 minutes to reheat.

Taste and adjust the seasoning with salt and pepper. Stir in the filé powder, then add the shrimp, stir to mix, re-cover, and cook on the low setting for 15 minutes. The shrimp should be opaque throughout.

Spoon the rice into individual shallow bowls, top with the gumbo, and serve.

Thickened with a deep, caramel-hued roux and scented with sassafras and tomatoes, this fragrant New Orleans gumbo packs a lot of flavor into a bowl.

VEGETABLES, GRAINS & LEGUMES

BELL PEPPERS STUFFED WITH QUINOA, BLACK BEANS & CORN

Stuffed peppers are old-fashioned—and nearly everyone likes them. Here, this longtime favorite has been given a modern Tex-Mex update with a stuffing of quinoa, black beans, chili powder, plenty of fresh cilantro, and sweet corn kernels. For a vegan version, leave out the cheese.

1 cup (170 g) quinoa, rinsed

2 cups (480 ml) water

Kosher salt and freshly ground pepper

6 or 7 red, yellow, or orange bell peppers, about 2 lb (900 g) total weight

1 can (15 oz/425 g) black beans, drained and rinsed

1 cup (170 g) fresh or frozen corn kernels

1 cup (225 g) store-bought tomato salsa

Grated zest of 1 lime, plus 1 lime, cut into 6 or 7 wedges, for serving

3 tablespoons fresh lime juice

1 tablespoon chili powder

1½ teaspoons ground cumin

½ teaspoon onion powder

½ teaspoon garlic powder

1 cup (120 g) shredded Monterey jack cheese

¼ cup (15 g) chopped fresh cilantro, plus more for garnish

Olive oil, for brushing

SERVES 6–7

In a saucepan, combine the quinoa, water, and ½ teaspoon salt and bring to a boil over high heat. Reduce the heat to low, cover, and cook for 15 minutes.

While the quinoa cooks, trim the peppers. Cut off the stem end of each pepper, then remove the core and seeds. Use a spoon to scrape away the ribs. Each pepper should be cup shaped and intact, and all of the peppers should fit together upright in a single layer in a slow cooker.

When the quinoa is ready, remove from the heat, uncover, stir to fluff the grains, then transfer to a bowl. Add the black beans, corn, salsa, lime zest, lime juice, chili powder, cumin, onion powder, garlic powder, and ½ teaspoon each salt and pepper to the quinoa and stir to combine. Stir in ½ cup (60 g) of the cheese and the cilantro.

Brush the inside of a slow cooker with oil. Stuff the peppers with the quinoa mixture, dividing it evenly and filling them full. Arrange the peppers in a single layer in the slow cooker. Cover and cook on the low setting for 3 hours.

Top each pepper with the remaining ½ cup (60 g) cheese, dividing it evenly. Re-cover and cook on the low setting for 1 hour longer. The peppers should be tender when pierced with a knife, the stuffing should be heated through, and the cheese should be melted.

Carefully remove the peppers from the slow cooker, garnish with cilantro, and serve.

BRAISED GARLICKY LEEKS WITH PROSCIUTTO & POACHED EGGS

When you braise leeks, they turn meltingly tender, making them an ideal base for paper-thin strips of prosciutto and a runny poached egg. A splash of vinegar and plenty of garlic add sharp, bright flavor. You can serve this simple yet satisfying dish for brunch, lunch, or dinner.

6 leeks, about 1 inch (2.5 cm) in diameter

8 cloves garlic, peeled but left whole

½ small yellow onion, chopped

½ cup (120 ml) dry white wine

½ cup (120 ml) chicken stock

2 tablespoons olive oil

2 tablespoons white wine vinegar

3 fresh flat-leaf parsley sprigs

1 bay leaf

Kosher salt and freshly ground pepper

3 oz (90 g) thinly sliced prosciutto, each torn lengthwise into 2 or 3 pieces

4 large eggs

3 tablespoons fresh small basil leaves

SERVES 4

Trim off the root end and then cut off the dark green tops from each leek, leaving about 2 inches (5 cm) of light green tops attached. Halve each leek lengthwise, rinse well, then cut crosswise into slices about ¾ inch (2 cm) thick. Transfer to a slow cooker.

Add the garlic, onion, wine, stock, oil, 1 tablespoon of the vinegar, parsley, bay leaf, ½ teaspoon salt, and several grinds of pepper and stir to mix. Cover and cook on the low setting for 3 hours, stirring once halfway during cooking if possible. The leeks should be very tender. Remove and discard the bay leaf and parsley sprigs. Re-cover to keep warm.

About 30 minutes before the leeks are ready, preheat an oven to 350°F (180°C). Lay the slices of prosciutto on a baking sheet in a single layer. Bake until firm and golden, 15–20 minutes. Let cool.

To poach the eggs, fill a large, deep sauté pan three-fourths full of water, bring to a rolling boil over high heat, and add the remaining 1 tablespoon vinegar. Crack an egg into a small ramekin or bowl. Reduce the heat to low and, holding the ramekin just above the surface of the barely simmering water, slide the egg into the water. Repeat with the remaining eggs, working as quickly as possible and keeping the eggs separated in the water. When all of the eggs are in the water, cover the pan and leave undisturbed for about 3 minutes if you like the yolks runny and 5 minutes if you like the yolks set.

Using a slotted spoon, divide the leek mixture among individual plates. Scatter the crispy prosciutto on top. Using the slotted spoon, place a poached egg on each bed of leeks. Sprinkle evenly with the basil and serve.

A softly poached egg adds rich creaminess to each bowl of slow-cooked leeks.

RED CURRY BUTTERNUT SQUASH SOUP WITH THAI BASIL

The simplicity of this soup belies its incredible flavor. Coconut milk adds creaminess, red curry paste gives it depth, lime juice brightens all of the flavors, and the lime leaves provide incomparable fragrance. Look for lime leaves in the produce or freezer section of a well-stocked Asian grocery store.

1 butternut squash, 3 lb (1.4 kg)

2 cups (480 ml) chicken or vegetable stock

1 can (14 fl oz/425 ml) coconut milk (not light), shaken well before opening

2 tablespoons fresh lime juice

¾ cup (75 g) sliced shallots

3 makrut (kaffir) lime leaves

2 tablespoons Thai red curry paste

1 teaspoon packed peeled and grated fresh ginger

1 clove garlic, minced

Kosher salt

Chopped fresh Thai basil, for garnish (optional)

SERVES 6–8

Peel the squash with a vegetable peeler, then halve through the stem end. Using a spoon, scoop out and discard the seeds. Cut the squash into 1-inch cubes.

Put the squash cubes, stock, coconut milk, lime juice, shallots, lime leaves, curry paste, ginger, garlic, and ⅛ teaspoon salt in a slow cooker and stir well. Cover and cook on the low setting for 6 hours. The squash should be very tender.

Uncover and let cool for a few minutes. Remove and discard the lime leaves. Working in batches if needed, transfer the contents of the slow cooker to a blender or food processor and process until a smooth purée forms. Return the soup to the slow cooker, cover, and heat on the low setting to warm through.

Taste and adjust the seasoni metal ng with salt and lime juice if needed. Ladle the soup into individual bowls, garnish with basil, if using, and serve.

SMOKY EGGPLANT DIP WITH PAPRIKA, LEMON & FETA

Similar in texture to baba ghanoush, a dip traditionally made by roasting whole eggplant then scooping out the soft interior, this party-ready spread gets its smoky flavor from smoked paprika, which can range from sweet to very spicy. Look for Italian eggplants, which are slimmer, smaller, and milder cousins to the globe eggplant.

2 lb (900 g) small Italian eggplants, peeled and cut into 1-inch (2.5-cm) pieces

¼ cup (60 ml) extra-virgin olive oil, plus more for serving

3 tablespoons fresh lemon juice

2 cloves garlic, minced

1 teaspoon smoked paprika

Kosher salt

¼ cup (60 g) tahini

1 tablespoon chopped fresh flat-leaf Italian parsley, plus more for garnish

1 tablespoon chopped fresh mint, plus more for garnish

¼ cup (35 g) crumbled feta cheese

Pita chips, homemade (page 133) or store-bought, for serving

SERVES 8–10

In a slow cooker, combine the eggplants, oil, lemon juice, garlic, paprika, and ½ teaspoon salt and stir and toss to mix well. Cover and cook on the high setting for 4½ hours. The eggplant should be very soft.

Stir the tahini into the eggplant mixture, then, using an immersion blender, process the dip to the consistency you like. (If you prefer a chunky texture, use a potato masher instead of a blender.) Transfer the dip to a serving bowl and let cool to room temperature. Stir in the parsley and mint, then taste and adjust the seasoning with salt and lemon juice if needed.

The dip can be served right away, or it can be covered and refrigerated for up to 5 days, then served chilled or at room temperature. Just before serving, drizzle with oil and sprinkle with parsley, mint, and the feta. Serve the pita chips alongside.

Za'atar is a Middle Eastern spice blend featuring its namesake herb, ground sumac, and ground sesame seeds, which give it a slightly nutty flavor.

HEIRLOOM CARROT HUMMUS WITH ZA'ATAR PITA CHIPS

If you like the creamy texture of hummus, you'll love this sweet-earthy version made entirely of carrots (no chickpeas here!). For a bright orange hummus, use only orange and red carrots; white and purple carrots will change the color. If only ordinary orange carrots are available, they will work, too. If you want more pita chips, just double the recipe and bake them in batches.

FOR THE HUMMUS

1¾–2 lb (800–900 g) heirloom carrots

3 tablespoons fresh lemon juice

2 tablespoons olive oil, plus more for drizzling

1 teaspoon firmly packed golden brown sugar

1 teaspoon ground cumin

½ teaspoon ground coriander

Kosher salt

¼ cup (60 g) tahini paste

Sweet paprika, for garnish

FOR THE ZA'ATAR PITA CHIPS

¼ cup (20 g) za'atar (see note at left)

7 tablespoons (105 ml) olive oil

2 white or whole-wheat pita breads, about 7 inches (18 cm) in diameter

Kosher salt

SERVES 8–10

To make the hummus, peel the carrots and cut them into 1-inch (2.5-cm) pieces; you should have about 1½ lb (680 g). Put the carrots in a slow cooker.

In a small bowl, whisk together the lemon juice, oil, sugar, cumin, coriander, and 1½ teaspoons salt. Pour the mixture over the carrots and stir to coat evenly. Cover and cook on the low setting for 5 hours. The carrots should be very tender.

Meanwhile, make the pita chips. Preheat the oven to 375°F (190°C). In a small bowl, stir together the za'atar and oil. Using a sharp paring knife, carefully split each pita open around the edge to create 4 separate rounds. Using a pastry brush, spread the za'atar oil evenly over the rough side of each pita round. Cut each round into 8 wedges (for a total of 32 chips) and arrange the wedges, brushed side up, in a single layer on a large rimmed baking sheet. Sprinkle the wedges with a little salt.

Bake until golden brown and crispy, about 7 minutes. Remove from the oven and let cool completely. (The chips can be stored in an airtight container at room temperature for up to 5 days.)

When the carrot mixture is ready, transfer to a food processor, add the tahini, and process until very smooth, stopping to scrape down the sides of the food processor with a rubber spatula once or twice. If the mixture is too thick, add a little water, 1 tablespoon at a time, until the consistency is more fluid. Taste and adjust the seasoning with salt and lemon juice if needed. You should have about 2 cups (450 g). (The hummus will keep in an airtight container in the refrigerator for up to 1 week.) Transfer to a serving bowl and let cool.

Drizzle the hummus with a little oil and sprinkle with paprika, then serve, with the pita chips alongside.

ARTICHOKES WITH GARLIC, LEMON, CHARD & TOMATOES

Artichokes become supple in a slow cooker. Here, they are paired with a filling of chard, garlic, tomatoes, and onion, plus creamy feta. Crunchy, garlicky bread crumbs—quickly toasted on the stove top—are strewn over the stuffing just before serving.

1 lemon, halved

4 globe artichokes

3 tablespoons olive oil

½ yellow onion, finely chopped

1 small bunch Swiss chard, stems removed and finely chopped and leaves thinly sliced crosswise

1½ teaspoons minced fresh rosemary

4 cloves garlic, sliced

3 tomatoes, halved, seeded, and diced

3 oz (90 g) feta cheese, crumbled

Kosher salt and freshly ground pepper

½ cup (120 ml) dry white wine

½ cup (120 ml) chicken stock

1 teaspoon white wine vinegar

FOR THE BREAD CRUMBS

3 cloves garlic

3 thick slices coarse country bread, crusts removed and torn into large pieces

Kosher salt

Freshly ground pepper

2 tablespoons olive oil

2 tablespoons chopped fresh flat-leaf parsley

SERVES 4

Fill a large bowl three-fourths full of cold water, squeeze in the lemon juice, and add the spent lemon halves. Working with 1 artichoke at a time, using a sharp knife, cut off the top one-third of the artichoke. Pull off and discard the tough outer leaves. Using scissors, snip off any prickly leaf tips that remain. Using the knife, trim any remnants of the tough leaves from the base of the artichoke, then remove the tough outer layer of the stem. Halve the artichoke lengthwise. Scoop out the hairy choke with a spoon. Drop the artichoke halves into the lemon water to prevent browning. Repeat with the remaining artichokes.

In a large, heavy frying pan over medium heat, warm the oil. Add the onion, chard stems, and rosemary and cook, stirring often, until the vegetables start to soften, about 6 minutes. Add the garlic and chard leaves and cook, stirring occasionally, until the leaves are wilted, about 5 minutes. Remove from the heat and stir in the tomatoes, cheese, ½ teaspoon salt, and several grinds of pepper.

Retrieve the artichoke halves from the lemon water (reserve the water) and place, cut side up, on a work surface. Mound the filling high in the center of each half, packing it firmly. Place the artichokes, stuffing side up, in a slow cooker. Drizzle the wine, stock, vinegar, and about 1 cup (240 ml) of the lemon water around the edges to reach to just below the cut surface of the artichokes. Cover and cook on the low setting for 5–6 hours. The artichokes are ready when the bases are tender when pierced with a knife tip.

Before serving, make the bread crumbs: Turn on a food processor, drop the garlic cloves through the feed tube, and process until finely chopped, about 10 seconds. Add the bread, ¼ teaspoon salt, and several grinds of pepper and process until coarse crumbs form. Drizzle in the oil and process until well mixed. Transfer the mixture to a large frying pan over medium heat and cook, stirring, until golden, 2–3 minutes. Remove from the heat, add the parsley, and toss to mix.

Using a slotted spoon, carefully lift the artichoke halves from the cooking liquid and place on a serving platter. Discard the cooking liquid. Scatter the bread crumbs over the artichokes and serve.

RUSTIC ITALIAN BEAN & FARRO SOUP

This peasant-style soup uses maroon-mottled cranberry beans, which become plump and creamy when cooked. If you cannot find them, pinto beans are a fine substitute. The beans are married with chewy farro, a flavorful nutrient-rich grain, to make this soup a welcome wintertime supper.

1 cup (200 g) dried cranberry beans, picked over and rinsed

3 tablespoons olive oil

1 large yellow onion, finely chopped

3 carrots, peeled, halved lengthwise, and cut crosswise into chunks

2 celery stalks, finely chopped

6 cloves garlic, sliced

6 cups (1.4 l) vegetable or chicken stock

2 fresh oregano sprigs

1 cup (205 g) semipearled farro, rinsed

1 can (15 oz/425 g) diced tomatoes, drained

2 teaspoons balsamic vinegar

1 teaspoon salt

Freshly ground pepper

6 oz (170 g) pancetta, thickly sliced, then chopped

1½ cups (45 g) baby spinach or arugula

Freshly shredded Parmesan cheese, for serving

SERVES 4–6

In a large bowl, combine the beans with water to cover by 2 inches (5 cm) and let soak overnight. Drain well.

In a large, heavy frying pan over medium-high heat, warm 2 tablespoons of the oil. Add the onion, carrots, and celery and cook, stirring often, until softened, about 6 minutes. Add the garlic and cook, stirring, for 1 minute longer. Pour in 1 cup (240 ml) of the stock and stir to dislodge any browned bits from the pan bottom.

Transfer the contents of the pan to a slow cooker. Stir in the drained beans, the remaining 5 cups (1.2 l) stock, and the oregano. Cover and cook on the low setting for 6 hours.

Stir in the farro, tomatoes, vinegar, salt, and several grinds of pepper, re-cover, and cook on the low setting for 2– 2½ hours longer. The beans should be tender and the farro should be tender but still slightly firm.

About 5 minutes before the soup is ready, in a heavy frying pan over medium heat, warm the remaining 1 tablespoon oil. Add the pancetta and cook, stirring often, until crisp and golden, about 4 minutes. Using a slotted spoon, transfer the pancetta to paper towels to drain.

Remove and discard the oregano sprigs, then taste and adjust the seasoning with salt and pepper if needed. Ladle the soup into shallow bowls. Top each serving with an equal amount of the spinach, garnish with the Parmesan and pancetta, and serve.

GREEK LENTIL SOUP WITH ROASTED PEPPERS & FETA

Red onion, garlic, roasted peppers, and a splash of red wine vinegar amp up the flavors in this tomato-laced lentil soup. The recipe calls for common brown lentils, but smaller French Puy (green) lentils can be substituted. They may need to cook a little longer. A garnish of salty-creamy feta cheese adds a rich note to each bowl.

¼ cup (60 ml) olive oil

1 red onion, finely chopped

3 cloves garlic, minced

1 tablespoon tomato paste

1 lb (450 g) brown lentils, picked over and rinsed

4 cups (950 ml) chicken stock

4 cups (950 ml) water

1 can (14½ oz/410 g) crushed tomatoes with juices

2 bay leaves

Kosher salt and freshly ground pepper

2 large jarred roasted red peppers, drained, seeded, and finely chopped (about 1 cup/170 g)

¼ cup (60 ml) red wine vinegar

About ⅓ cup (50 g) crumbled feta

¼ cup (15 g) chopped fresh flat-leaf Italian parsley

SERVES 6–8

In a frying pan over medium heat, warm the oil. Add the onion and garlic and cook, stirring often, until softened, about 5 minutes. Stir in the tomato paste, mixing well.

Scrape the onion mixture into the slow cooker. Add the lentils, stock, water, crushed tomatoes with their juices, bay leaves, 2 teaspoons salt, and ½ teaspoon pepper and stir to mix. Cover and cook on the low setting for 6 hours, stirring once halfway during cooking if possible. The lentils should be tender.

Stir in the roasted peppers and vinegar, re-cover, and continue to cook for 30 minutes longer to blend the flavors. Taste and adjust the seasoning with salt and pepper if needed.

Ladle the soup into individual bowls, top with the feta and parsley, and serve.

Turmeric contributes color, warm and earthy flavor, and subtle health benefits to this silky soup.

CAULIFLOWER-TURMERIC SOUP WITH TOASTED ALMONDS

This silky smooth, brilliant yellow soup is tasty and nourishing and can easily be made vegan. Cauliflower and potatoes create a hearty base, and spices, garlic, ginger, and lemon add layers of flavor. Don't skimp on the garnishes. The fresh cilantro and toasted almonds contribute a pretty finish and a crunchy texture.

1 head cauliflower, about 2½ lb (1.1 kg)

1 lb (450 g) Yukon gold potatoes (about 4), peeled and cut into 1-inch (2.5-cm) cubes

2 tablespoons coconut oil, ghee, or olive oil

1 small yellow onion, finely chopped

3 cloves garlic, minced

1 tablespoon peeled and grated fresh ginger

1 tablespoon firmly packed golden brown sugar (optional)

1 tablespoon ground turmeric

2 teaspoons ground cumin

1 teaspoon ground coriander

½–1 teaspoon cayenne pepper (optional)

Kosher salt and freshly ground black pepper

1 can (14 fl oz/425 ml) coconut milk (not light), shaken well before opening

2 cups (480 ml) chicken or vegetable stock or water

Juice of ½ lemon

¼ cup (15 g) chopped fresh cilantro, plus more for garnish

⅓ cup (30 g) sliced almonds, toasted

SERVES 6

Trim the cauliflower and cut into equal-size florets, each about 1½ inches (4 cm). (You should have about 1½ lb/680 g.) Put the cauliflower and potatoes in a slow cooker.

In a frying pan over medium heat, warm the coconut oil. Add the onion and garlic and cook, stirring often, until lightly golden, about 7 minutes. Add the ginger, sugar (if using), turmeric, cumin, coriander, cayenne to taste (if using), 2 teaspoons salt, and ½ teaspoon black pepper, stir to combine, and let cook for 30 seconds. Add the coconut milk and stir until the coconut solids have melted. Remove from the heat.

Pour the coconut milk mixture and the stock into the slow cooker and stir to mix with the vegetables. Cover and cook on the low setting for 6 hours, stirring once or twice if possible. The vegetables should be very tender.

Uncover, let cool for a few minutes, then stir in the lemon juice and cilantro. Using a ladle, transfer the mixture to a blender or food processor and process until smooth. (You may need to purée the soup in batches, depending on the size of your blender or processor.) Return the soup to the slow cooker, re-cover, and heat on the low setting until warmed through, 15–30 minutes. Taste and adjust the seasoning with salt and pepper.

Ladle the soup into individual bowls. Top each bowl with a sprinkle of cilantro, toasted almonds, and a few grinds of black pepper, then serve.

CARAMELIZED ONION SOUP WITH GRUYÈRE TOASTS

No more standing at the stove top stirring onions for an hour to make this classic French soup. The slow cooker does all the work for you! Sherry adds fragrance and flavor to the soup, but you can also use white wine if that's what you have on hand. Nutty-flavored Gruyère, a good melting cheese, makes exceptional toasts. Be sure to garnish with plenty of parsley to add a fresh note.

FOR THE CARAMELIZED ONIONS

4 large yellow onions, halved and thinly sliced

4 tablespoons (60 g) unsalted butter, melted

Kosher salt

¼ cup (60 ml) dry white wine

¼ cup (60 ml) medium-dry sherry

5 cups (1.2 l) beef stock

2 fresh thyme sprigs

12 slices baguette, cut on the diagonal

½ cup (60 g) freshly grated Parmesan or Gruyère cheese

3 tablespoons finely snipped fresh chives

SERVES 4–6

To make the caramelized onions, the night before serving, put the onions in a slow cooker, add the butter and 1 teaspoon salt, and toss to coat the onions evenly. Cover and cook on the low setting for 10 hours, stirring once in the first few hours if possible. The next morning, stir the onions, re-cover, and cook on the high setting until the onions are golden and most of the liquid has evaporated, 1–2 hours. If the liquid has not evaporated, set the lid ajar for 1–2 hours to evaporate the liquid while the onions continue to cook. (The onions can be caramelized in advance. Let cool to room temperature, then transfer to an airtight container and refrigerate for up to 3 days or freeze for up to 3 months.)

When the onions are ready, add the white wine, sherry, stock, and thyme to the onions and stir well. Cover and cook on the low setting for 5 hours. The onions should be very soft.

Just before the soup is ready, preheat the broiler. Arrange the baguette slices on a rimmed baking sheet and top them with the cheese, arranging it in an even layer. Broil until the tops are golden, about 30 seconds.

Remove and discard the thyme sprigs from the soup. Ladle the soup into shallow bowls, top each serving with 2 or 3 Gruyère toasts, sprinkle with the chives, and serve.

CREAMY HERBED POLENTA WITH WILD MUSHROOMS

Thick, creamy polenta makes a wonderful base for braised meats, Bolognese sauce (page 40), Roasted Root Vegetables (page 174), or for the earthy, garlicky mushrooms included here. Because the polenta simmers unattended in a slow cooker, unlike its stove-top counterpart, it becomes a savvy option for a busy weeknight dinner.

4 cups (950 ml) chicken stock

1 cup (155 g) stone-ground polenta

Salt and freshly ground pepper

1 tablespoon unsalted butter

1 tablespoon olive oil

¾ lb (340 g) mixed wild mushrooms, brushed clean, stem ends trimmed, and quartered

1 large shallot, finely chopped

3 cloves garlic, minced

2 tablespoons coarsely chopped fresh flat-leaf parsley

2 teaspoons minced fresh oregano, plus more for garnish

2 teaspoons minced fresh thyme, plus more for garnish

½ cup (60 g) freshly grated Parmesan cheese

1 cup (170 g) fresh or thawed frozen corn kernels

SERVES 4–6

In a slow cooker, stir together the stock, polenta, 1 teaspoon salt, and several grinds of pepper. Cover and cook on the low setting for 3–3½ hours, stirring two or three times during cooking if possible. The liquid should be absorbed and the polenta should be thick and soft and no longer gritty.

About 10 minutes before the polenta is ready, in a large, heavy frying pan over medium-high heat, melt the butter with the oil. Add the mushrooms and shallot and cook, stirring often, until the mushrooms are tender and the liquid they release has evaporated, about 5 minutes. Stir in the garlic and parsley, season with salt and pepper, and cook for 1 minute longer. Keep warm.

About 5 minutes before the polenta is ready, add the oregano, thyme, Parmesan, and corn kernels to the polenta and stir well. Re-cover and continue to cook for 5 minutes.

Spoon the polenta into individual shallow bowls or a serving bowl and top with the mushroom mixture. Garnish the polenta and mushrooms with oregano and thyme and serve.

CREAMED BRUSSELS SPROUTS WITH BACON & GRUYÈRE

The low, steady heat of a slow cooker yields tender, flavorful brussels sprouts that hold their shape. Here, the mildly bitter sprouts are paired with a rich Gruyère cheese–based sauce studded with salty bacon. Serve this warming dish alongside roasted meat and potatoes on a wintry evening.

2 lb (900 g) small, tender brussels sprouts, ends trimmed and halved lengthwise

¼ lb (120 g) applewood smoked bacon, diced

2 tablespoons unsalted butter

3 large shallots, thinly sliced

¼ cup (30 g) all-purpose flour

1½ cups (350 ml) chicken stock

1 cup (240 ml) whole milk

1 cup (170 g) firmly packed shredded Gruyère cheese (about 6 oz)

Kosher salt and freshly ground pepper

SERVES 8–10

Put the brussels sprouts in a slow cooker.

In a frying pan over medium heat, fry the bacon, stirring occasionally, until crisp, about 5 minutes. Using a slotted spoon, transfer the bacon to paper towels to drain.

Pour off all but 1 tablespoon fat in the pan, return the pan to medium heat, and melt the butter. Add the shallots and cook, stirring often, until they start to soften, about 2 minutes. Sprinkle the flour over the shallots and stir to coat evenly. Slowly add the stock and then the milk while stirring constantly. Continue to cook, stirring, until the mixture thickens, about 1 minute. Add the cheese, reserved bacon, 1 teaspoon salt, and ½ teaspoon pepper and stir until the cheese melts. Remove from the heat.

Pour the cheese sauce over the sprouts and stir to combine; the mixture will be thick. Cover and cook on the low setting for about 3½ hours, stirring a few times during cooking if possible. The sprouts should be tender.

Give the sprouts and sauce a stir, then taste and adjust the seasoning with salt and pepper if needed. Transfer to a serving dish and serve.

MEDITERRANEAN RATATOUILLE WITH PARMESAN POLENTA

Looking for a good way to use up your bountiful harvest of summertime vegetables—and a good reason to use your slow cooker in July? Ratatouille is equally delicious served hot, warm, or at room temperature, and it tastes even better after a day in the refrigerator. Serve it hot over creamy polenta (as here) or on its own as a flavorful side.

1 lb (450 g) small eggplants, cut into 1-inch (2.5-cm) pieces

Kosher salt and freshly ground pepper

3 tablespoons tomato paste

3 tablespoons olive oil, plus more for drizzling

4 cloves garlic, finely chopped

1 teaspoon dried oregano

1 large yellow onion, halved and thinly sliced

2 red bell peppers, seeded and cut lengthwise into narrow strips

3 zucchini, trimmed, halved lengthwise, and cut crosswise ⅓ inch (9 mm) thick

4 plum tomatoes, quartered lengthwise and seeded

Creamy Parmesan Polenta (page 173)

¼ cup (15 g) fresh flat-leaf parsley leaves, finely chopped

3 tablespoons coarsely chopped fresh basil leaves

⅓ cup (55 g) capers, rinsed

SERVES 4–6

In a colander, toss the eggplant with 1 teaspoon salt, then let drain for about 30 minutes. Pat dry with paper towels.

In a small bowl, whisk together the tomato paste, oil, garlic, oregano, 1 teaspoon salt, and several grinds of pepper.

Add the eggplant, onion, bell peppers, zucchini, and tomatoes to a slow cooker. Spoon the tomato paste mixture over the top and stir well to coat evenly. Cover and cook on the low setting for 5 hours, stirring once or twice during cooking if possible.

About 30 minutes before the ratatouille is done, cook the polenta.

Divide the polenta among individual serving bowls. Add the parsley to the ratatouille and stir until well mixed, then spoon the ratatouille evenly over each bowl of polenta. Sprinkle each serving evenly with the basil and capers, drizzle with a little oil, and serve.

FARRO WITH SPRING VEGETABLES

Farro, an ancient wheat strain still used in Italian kitchens, holds its shape as it cooks, making it ideal for soups, salads, or side dishes. In this springtime dish, it is paired with asparagus, peas, and leeks, plus plenty of fresh herbs and salty shaved Parmesan, to create a light, healthy main dish or a hearty side to grilled chicken or steak.

3 tablespoons olive oil

½ yellow onion, finely chopped

2 celery stalks, finely chopped

2 oz (60 g) pancetta, diced

1½ cups (310 g) semipearled farro, rinsed

½ cup (120 ml) dry white wine

4 cups (950 ml) chicken stock

Kosher salt and freshly ground pepper

1 lb (450 g) asparagus, tough ends removed and spears cut into 2-inch (5-cm) lengths

1 tablespoon unsalted butter

2 leeks, white and pale green parts, cut into 2-inch (5-cm) matchsticks

2 cups (285 g) fresh or thawed, frozen English peas

Grated zest and juice of ½ lemon

2 tablespoons chopped fresh flat-leaf parsley

3-oz (90-g) piece Parmesan cheese

SERVES 6

In a large frying pan over medium heat, warm 2 tablespoons of the oil. Add the onion, celery, and pancetta and cook, stirring occasionally, until the onion has softened and the pancetta has rendered most of its fat, about 6 minutes. Add the farro, stir to coat with the oil, and cook, stirring, until lightly toasted, 1–2 minutes. Add the wine and stir until it has evaporated, about 5 minutes. Pour in 1 cup (240 ml) of the stock and stir to dislodge any browned bits from the pan bottom.

Transfer the contents of the pan to a slow cooker. Stir in the remaining 3 cups (700 ml) stock, ½ teaspoon salt, and several grinds of pepper. Cover and cook on the low setting for 2–2½ hours. The farro should be tender.

While the farro is cooking, bring a saucepan three-fourths full of salted water to a boil, add the asparagus and cook until tender-crisp, 2–4 minutes. Drain and rinse under cold running water until cool. Spread on a kitchen towel to dry.

About 5 minutes before the farro is ready, in a frying pan over medium heat, melt the butter with the remaining 1 tablespoon oil. Add the leeks and cook, stirring occasionally, for 2 minutes. Add the peas and cook, stirring, for 2 minutes. Add the asparagus and cook, stirring, until heated through, 1–2 minutes longer. Stir in the lemon juice.

Stir the vegetables into the farro and transfer to a warm serving dish. Garnish with the lemon zest and parsley. Using a vegetable peeler, shave the Parmesan over the top, then serve.

A sprinkling of grated
lemon zest and finely
chopped parsley adds
fresh flavor to each
bowl just before serving.

MEYER LEMON BARLEY RISOTTO WITH CHOPPED GREENS

Made in the style of risotto, this creamy barley dish gets loads of flavor from tart-sweet Meyer lemons and plenty of sautéed shallots. The shallots are cooked briefly on the stove top to soften their bite before they join the remaining ingredients in the slow cooker. For a heartier meal, add sautéed asparagus or shrimp.

2 Meyer lemons

2 tablespoons unsalted butter

2 shallots, finely chopped
(½ cup/80 g)

1½ cups (300 g) pearl barley

5 cups (1.2 l) chicken or
vegetable stock, plus more
if needed

½ cup (120 ml) dry white wine

Kosher salt and freshly
ground pepper

3 cups (90 g) baby spinach,
roughly chopped

¼ cup (15 g) chopped fresh
flat-leaf parsley

¼ cup (35 g) pine nuts, toasted

½ cup (60 g) freshly grated
Parmesan cheese, plus small
chunk for serving

Extra-virgin olive oil,
for serving

SERVES 4–6

Grate the zest from 1 Meyer lemon, then halve and juice the lemon. Reserve the remaining lemon.

In a small frying pan over medium heat, melt the butter. Add the shallots and cook, stirring, until beginning to soften, about 2 minutes.

Scrape the shallots into a slow cooker. Add the barley, 4 cups (950 ml) of the stock, the wine, lemon zest and juice, 1 teaspoon salt, and ¼ teaspoon pepper and stir to combine. Cover and cook on the low setting for 3 hours. The barley should be tender but still a little chewy.

Just before the barley is ready, in a bowl, toss together the spinach, parsley, and pine nuts, mixing well.

Warm the remaining 1 cup (240 ml) stock in a microwave or on the stove top until hot. Stir the warm stock and grated Parmesan into the barley. The mixture should be creamy, like risotto; if it is not, add more warm stock to achieve the desired consistency. Taste the risotto and adjust the seasoning with salt, pepper, and lemon juice if needed.

Spoon the barley risotto into individual wide, shallow bowls. Top each serving with an equal amount of the spinach mixture and drizzle with a little oil. Using a vegetable peeler, shave shards of Parmesan over the top and serve. Cut the remaining lemon into wedges and pass at the table.

VEGETABLE LASAGNA WITH SPINACH, MUSHROOMS & RICOTTA

This vegetarian lasagna checks all the boxes: hearty and rich, with layers of creamy ricotta, noodles, and tomato sauce chunky with cremini mushrooms, fresh spinach, and bell peppers. Add 1 diced Asian eggplant with the mushrooms for even more variety, if you like. For a meat lasagna, try the beef and squash lasagna on page 38.

1 tablespoon olive oil

1 small yellow onion, finely chopped

¾ lb (340 g) cremini mushrooms, brushed clean, stem ends trimmed, and chopped

1 large carrot, peeled and shredded

6 oz (170 g) baby spinach, chopped, or 2 zucchini, trimmed and cut into ½-inch (12-mm) dice

3 cans (14½ oz/410 g each) crushed tomatoes, with juices

1 jar (12 oz/340 g) roasted red peppers (about 3 peppers), drained and chopped

1 cup (30 g) fresh basil leaves, finely chopped

Kosher salt and freshly ground pepper

1 container (15 oz/425 g) whole-milk ricotta cheese (2 cups)

¾ cup (90 g) freshly grated Parmesan cheese

1 large egg, lightly beaten

Grated zest of 1 lemon

9 dried lasagna noodles (do not use "no-boil" noodles)

½ lb (225 g) shredded whole-milk mozzarella cheese

SERVES 8

In a large frying pan over medium heat, warm the oil. Add the onion and cook, stirring occasionally, until softened, about 6 minutes. Add the mushrooms and carrot and cook, stirring often, until tender, about 7 minutes. Add the spinach and cook, stirring, until wilted, about 1 minute. Stir in the tomatoes, red peppers, basil, and ¼ cup (60 ml) water, season with salt and pepper, and remove from the heat. You should have about 8 cups (1.9 l) sauce.

In a bowl, stir together the ricotta, ½ cup (55 g) of the Parmesan, the egg, lemon zest, and a generous pinch each of salt and pepper.

Spread 2 cups (475 ml) of the sauce on the bottom of the slow cooker. Cover the sauce with 3 uncooked lasagna noodles, breaking the noodles and overlapping them slightly as needed to fit in a single layer. Spread 1 cup (240 ml) of the sauce evenly over the noodles. Dollop half of the ricotta mixture over the sauce, then top with ½ cup (55 g) of the mozzarella and 1 cup (240 ml) of the sauce. Repeat the layers, starting with 3 noodles, then 1 cup (240 ml) of the sauce, the remaining ricotta mixture, ½ cup (55 g) of the mozzarella, and 1 cup (240 ml) of the sauce. Top the sauce with a third layer of noodles, then the remaining 2 cups (475 ml) sauce. Top evenly with the remaining 1 cup (115 g) mozzarella and the remaining ¼ cup (30 g) Parmesan.

Cover and cook on the low setting for 4 hours. The lasagna noodles should be cooked through and tender.

Uncover, taking care not to let the condensation on the lid drip back onto the lasagna. Let stand for 10 minutes before serving directly from the slow cooker.

Look for small black lentils, sometimes called beluga lentils, in specialty food stores, South Asian markets, and many supermarkets.

PUNJABI-STYLE BLACK LENTIL DAL

Enriched with cream and butter, decadent Punjabi-style dal—called *dal makhani*—is a celebratory lentil dish from northern India. Kidney beans are a common addition to *dal makhani*; if you like, add 1 can (15 oz/425 g) kidney beans, drained and rinsed, during the last hour of cooking. Offer warm naan or fresh chapatis (as here) for serving.

5 tablespoons (75 g) unsalted butter

1 small yellow onion, finely chopped

1 tablespoon peeled and shredded fresh ginger

3 cloves garlic, minced

3 tablespoons tomato paste

2 teaspoons ancho or other medium-hot chile powder

2 teaspoons garam masala

1 teaspoon ground cumin

1 teaspoon ground coriander

½ teaspoon ground cinnamon

½ teaspoon ground fennel

¼ teaspoon ground cardamom

¼ teaspoon ground cloves

Kosher salt

5 cups (1.2 l) water

1 lb (450 g) black (beluga) lentils, rinsed

2 bay leaves

2 star anise pods

2 cups (480 ml) low-sodium chicken or vegetable stock

¼ cup (60 ml) heavy cream, plus more to finish

¼ cup (15 g) chopped fresh cilantro

SERVES 8

In a frying pan over medium heat, melt 2 tablespoons of the butter. Add the onion, ginger, and garlic and cook, stirring often, until softened, about 6 minutes. Stir in the tomato paste, mixing well, then add the chile powder, garam masala, cumin, coriander, cinnamon, fennel, cardamom, cloves, and 1½ teaspoons salt. Add 1 cup (240 ml) of the water, stir well to combine, bring to a simmer, and remove from the heat.

Scrape the spice mixture into the slow cooker, add the lentils, bay leaves, and star anise, and then pour in the stock and the remaining 4 cups (950 ml) water and stir to mix well. Cover and cook on the low setting for 8 hours. The lentils should be very tender.

Stir in the cream and the remaining 3 tablespoons butter until melted. Taste and adjust the seasoning with salt if needed. Ladle into individual bowls, drizzle with a little cream, sprinkle with cilantro, and serve.

SPICED ACORN SQUASH WITH GARLIC-MINT-YOGURT SAUCE

Tender, mildly sweet acorn squash can be an easy side dish to roasted meats or a satisfying main course when served with quinoa, brown rice, or other whole grains. The bonus is that you don't even have to peel it. The simple yogurt sauce, flecked with mint and garlic, is a cool counterpoint to the winter vegetable.

1 acorn squash, 2½ lb (1.1 kg)

½ cup (120 ml) canola oil

1-inch (2.5-cm) piece fresh ginger, peeled and grated

1 teaspoon ground coriander

½ teaspoon ground cinnamon

½ teaspoon red pepper flakes

1 can (14½ oz/410 g) tomato sauce

½ cup (100 g) sugar

Kosher salt and freshly ground pepper

FOR THE YOGURT SAUCE

1 cup (225 g) plain whole-milk Greek yogurt

1–2 cloves garlic, minced

3 tablespoons chopped fresh mint

Kosher salt

SERVES 4–6

Using a large knife, cut the squash in half lengthwise. Scoop out the seeds with a large spoon, then cut the squash into 1½-inch (4-cm) pieces.

In a large, heavy frying pan over medium-high heat, warm the oil. Working in batches if needed to avoid crowding, add the squash and cook, stirring occasionally, until evenly browned, about 7 minutes. Using a slotted spoon, transfer to a slow cooker.

Add the ginger, coriander, cinnamon, and red pepper flakes to the frying pan and cook, stirring, until fragrant, about 30 seconds. Stir in the tomato sauce, sugar, ½ teaspoon salt, and a few grinds of pepper, bring to a boil, and remove from the heat.

Transfer the contents of the pan to the slow cooker and stir to mix well. Cover and cook for 4 hours on the low setting or 2 hours on the high setting. The squash should be very tender.

Meanwhile, make the yogurt sauce. In a bowl, stir together the yogurt, garlic, mint, and ½ teaspoon salt. Cover and refrigerate until serving.

Spoon the squash and its sauce onto a platter or individual plates. Serve with the yogurt sauce dolloped on top. Pass the remaining sauce at the table.

For a main course
rendition of this dish,
spoon mounds of the
spiced squash over
bowls of Steamed
Brown Rice (page 173).

SWEET POTATOES WITH HONEY & LIME

A squeeze of lime juice and a drizzle of honey bring out the natural sweetness of these popular cool-weather vegetables. Look for orange-fleshed sweet potatoes, commonly labeled "yams," which have the best flavor. If you like, add some crumbled *queso fresco* or a drizzle of *crema* or sour cream along with the cilantro.

2 lb (900 g) orange-fleshed sweet potatoes, peeled and cut into 1-inch (2.5-cm) chunks

3 tablespoons honey, warmed until free-flowing, plus more for drizzling (optional)

½ teaspoon white wine vinegar

½ teaspoon ground cumin

½ teaspoon ground cinnamon

Grated zest and juice of 1 lime

½ cup (120 ml) apple juice, preferably unfiltered, or water

Kosher salt and freshly ground pepper

2 tablespoons coarsely chopped fresh cilantro

SERVES 4–6

In a slow cooker, combine the sweet potatoes, honey, vinegar, cumin, cinnamon, lime zest and juice, apple juice, ¼ teaspoon salt, and several grinds of pepper and stir to mix well. Cover and cook on the low setting for about 4½ hours, stirring once or twice during cooking if possible. The sweet potatoes should be very tender.

Transfer to a serving dish. If desired, drizzle a little more honey over the sweet potatoes, then scatter the cilantro over the top and serve.

SLOW-COOKED ROASTED GARLIC MASHED POTATOES

These potatoes are kept extra light by slowly cooking them in broth, then adding whole milk or half-and-half in lieu of cream. You can omit the roasted garlic if you prefer plain mashed potatoes. To make herb mashed potatoes, omit the garlic and stir in 1 tablespoon chopped fresh chives, oregano, or basil, or a mix, just before serving.

5 lb (2.3 kg) Yukon gold or russet potatoes, peeled and cut into 1-inch (2.5-cm) pieces

1 cup (240 ml) chicken or vegetable stock

6 tablespoons (90 g) unsalted butter, cut into ½-inch (12-mm) pieces

Kosher salt and freshly ground pepper

1 large head garlic

Olive oil, for drizzling

About 1½ cups (350 ml) whole milk or half-and-half

SERVES 8–10

In a slow cooker, combine the potatoes, stock, butter, and 2 teaspoons salt and stir to mix. Cover and cook on the low setting for 5–6 hours, stirring a few times during cooking if possible. The potatoes should be very soft.

Meanwhile, preheat the oven to 325°F (165°C). Cut about ¼ inch (6 mm) off the top of the garlic head to expose the tops of the cloves. Drizzle the cut surface with a little oil, wrap the head in aluminum foil, and set the packet in a small baking dish. Bake until the garlic is very soft when a center clove is pierced with a small knife, about 1 hour.

Set the garlic aside to cool slightly, then separate the cloves and squeeze them into a small bowl, discarding their papery sheaths. Using a fork, mash them to a purée. (The garlic purée can be made up to 3 days in advance; cover and refrigerate until needed.)

When the potatoes are ready, warm the milk on the stove top or in a microwave until hot. Add 1 cup (240 ml) of the hot milk and the garlic purée to the potatoes, then mash with a potato masher to the consistency you like, adding more of the hot milk as needed. If you prefer whipped potatoes, use a dinner fork to beat them to a creamy consistency. Taste and adjust the seasoning with salt and pepper if needed.

Transfer the mashed potatoes to a serving dish and serve, or keep warm in the slow cooker on the warm setting until ready to serve.

DESSERTS

A slow cooker takes the
place of a traditional
bain-marie in preparing
these gently spiced
chocolate custards.

CHOCOLATE-CHILE POTS DE CRÈME

These sweet individual puddings may look innocent, but they pack a nicely spicy punch from the addition of ancho chile to the custard base. They are a perfect make-ahead dessert for anyone who likes the pairing of chiles and chocolate. Serve them topped with a dollop of whipped cream and a sprinkle of chile powder.

1½ cups (350 ml)
half-and-half

3 tablespoons sugar

⅛ teaspoon kosher salt

1 ancho chile, torn into
a few pieces

3 oz (90 g) good-quality
semisweet chocolate
(60 percent cacao), chopped

1 teaspoon pure vanilla
extract

4 large egg yolks

Whipped cream, for serving

Ancho chile powder,
for garnish

SERVES 4

Have ready 4 custard cups or ramekins, each about ½ cup (120 ml), that will fit in your slow cooker in a single layer.

In a small saucepan over medium heat, stir together the half-and-half, sugar, and salt until the mixture is steaming and the sugar has dissolved. Add the ancho chile, cover, and set aside to steep for 30 minutes.

Bring a kettle of water to a boil. Remove and discard the chile from the half-and-half. Add the chocolate to the half-and-half mixture and stir until the chocolate melts, then stir in the vanilla. In a large measuring pitcher, whisk the egg yolks just to break them up. Whisking constantly, pour the chocolate mixture into the yolks, stirring until well combined.

Pour the chocolate mixture through a fine-mesh sieve into the custard cups, dividing it evenly. Place the cups in the slow cooker. Pour boiling water into the slow cooker to reach about halfway up the sides of the cups, being careful not to splash any water on the custards. Wrap the slow cooker lid with a clean kitchen towel, cover the cooker (making sure the kitchen towel is pulled taut), and cook on the low setting for 1 hour. The custards should be set but still a little jiggly in the center when the cups are shaken.

Carefully transfer the custards to a wire rack and let cool completely. Cover the cups tightly with plastic wrap, making sure it doesn't touch the tops of the custards. Refrigerate until thoroughly chilled, at least 2 hours or up to 2 days.

Serve the custards with a dollop of whipped cream and a sprinkle of chile powder.

SALTED CARAMEL CRÈME BRÛLÉE

The slow cooker is well suited to nearly any dessert that calls for gentle cooking in a water bath, such as this deeply golden, salty-sweet crème brûlée. The recipe comes together quickly, and it can be made and refrigerated up to a day in advance. Melt the sugar just before serving and your elegant dinner-party dessert is ready for the table.

⅓ cup (70 g) granulated sugar

2 tablespoons water

1½ cups (350 ml) heavy cream

½ teaspoon kosher salt

4 large egg yolks

4 teaspoons raw sugar, such as demerara or turbinado

SERVES 4

Have ready 4 custard cups or ramekins, each about ½ cup (120 ml) capacity, that will fit in your slow cooker in a single layer.

Bring a kettle of water to a boil. In a small, heavy saucepan over medium-high heat, gently stir together the granulated sugar and water, then bring the mixture to a boil and cook, swirling the pan occasionally for even cooking (but do not stir), until an amber brown caramel forms. Reduce the heat to medium-low and carefully add the cream and salt (the cream will spatter), stirring until the caramel melts into the cream. Remove from the heat.

In a large, heatproof measuring pitcher, whisk the egg yolks just to break them up. Whisking constantly, slowly add the hot cream mixture to the yolks, continuing to whisk until well combined. Pour the mixture through a fine-mesh sieve into the custard cups, dividing it evenly. Place the cups in the slow cooker. Pour boiling water into the slow cooker to reach about halfway up the sides of the cups. Cover and cook on the low setting for 1–1½ hours. The custards should be set but still jiggle a little in the center when the cups are shaken.

Carefully transfer the custards to a wire rack and let cool completely. Cover the cups tightly with plastic wrap and refrigerate until thoroughly chilled, at least 2 hours or up to 2 days.

Just before serving, position an oven rack at the top of the oven and preheat the broiler. Sprinkle each custard with 1 teaspoon of the raw sugar, covering the surface with a thin, even layer. Place the custards on a rimmed baking sheet and slide under the broiler; the custards should be no more than 3 inches (7.5 cm) from the heat source. Within a few minutes, the sugar will melt and caramelize, turning a deep golden brown. Watch carefully to prevent burning. (Alternatively, use a kitchen torch to caramelize the sugar.)

Remove the custards from the broiler and let stand until the tops have cooled and hardened, then serve.

WARM CHOCOLATE BUDINO CAKE

A *budino*, or "pudding" in Italian, is a rich dessert that is sometimes more of a pudding and sometimes more of a cake. This recipe delivers a luscious dessert that is a balance of both, with a layer of ultramoist chocolate cake atop a deeply decadent, pudding-like hot fudge sauce. Serve with unsweetened whipped cream to cut the richness.

6 tablespoons (90 g) unsalted butter, plus more for the insert

1 cup (120 g) all-purpose flour

1 cup (200 g) sugar

⅔ cup (60 g) unsweetened cocoa powder, sifted

2 teaspoons baking powder

½ teaspoon kosher salt

3 oz (90 g) bittersweet chocolate, chopped

⅔ cup (160 ml) whole milk

2 teaspoons pure vanilla extract

1 cup (240 ml) brewed coffee, cold

Whipped cream or vanilla ice cream, for serving

SERVES 8

Butter the insert of a slow cooker evenly.

In a bowl, whisk together the flour, ½ cup (100 g) of the sugar, ⅓ cup (30 g) of the cocoa, the baking powder, and the salt. In a small saucepan over medium-low heat, melt together the 6 tablespoons butter and the chocolate, then whisk in the milk and vanilla until smooth. Pour the chocolate mixture into the flour mixture and stir until well mixed. Scrape the batter into the prepared slow cooker insert and, using a rubber spatula, smooth into an even layer.

In a bowl, whisk together the remaining ½ cup (100 g) sugar and ⅓ cup (30 g) cocoa. Sprinkle the sugar-cocoa mixture in an even layer over the surface of the batter. Gently pour the coffee evenly over the surface of the cocoa-topped batter. Do not stir.

Wrap the slow cooker lid with a clean kitchen towel, cover the cooker (making sure the kitchen towel is pulled taut), and cook on the low setting for about 2½ hours. The cake should be set along the edges and over most of the top surface except for the very center. Watch carefully toward the end of cooking to make sure the cake does not scorch. Turn off the slow cooker and let stand, covered, for at least 30 minutes and up to 1 hour.

Scoop the warm cake into shallow dessert bowls, top each serving with a scoop of ice cream, and serve.

GINGERSNAP-BRANDY CHEESECAKE

For this dessert, you'll need a 6-inch (15-cm) springform pan with 3-inch (7.5-cm) sides that will fit in your slow cooker. Finding it may take some sleuthing, but this cake is worth the search. This cheesecake can be made a day in advance of serving—and tastes even better when left out for a day. Use a food processor for the gingersnap crumbs.

FOR THE CRUST

Unsalted butter for greasing pan, plus 2 tablespoons unsalted butter, melted

1 cup (120 g) gingersnap crumbs (about 4 oz/115 g)

¼ teaspoon kosher salt

FOR THE FILLING

¾ lb (340 g) cream cheese, at room temperature

½ cup (100 g) sugar

½ teaspoon kosher salt

¼ teaspoon ground ginger

2 large eggs

2 tablespoons brandy

½ cup (120 g) sour cream

Blackberries, for serving (optional)

SERVES 6–8

Lightly butter a 6-inch (15-cm) springform pan with 3-inch (7.5-cm) sides (make sure the pan will fit in your slow cooker). Wrap the outside tightly with two layers of aluminum foil. If you have a small, short (about ½ inch/12 mm tall) wire rack that fits inside your slow cooker, place it on the bottom of the cooker. Otherwise, create a rack by making a "rope" of aluminum foil by twisting it into a coil and then setting it on the bottom.

To make the crust, in a small bowl, stir together the gingersnap crumbs, 2 tablespoons butter, and the salt until well mixed and the crumbs are evenly moistened. Press the mixture onto the bottom of the prepared springform pan. Set aside.

To make the filling, in a stand mixer fitted with the paddle attachment, beat together the cream cheese, sugar, salt, and ginger on medium-high speed until well mixed and smooth. Add the eggs, one at a time, beating after each addition until incorporated and then scraping down the bowl sides with a rubber spatula. After the second egg, beat the batter until smooth. Add the brandy and then the sour cream and beat until incorporated. Scrape down the bowl sides and then beat the batter again until smooth. Scrape the batter into the prepared pan and smooth the top.

Place the pan on the rack in the slow cooker and add warm water to come up to the bottom of the pan (about ½ inch/12 mm). Wrap the slow cooker lid with a clean kitchen towel, cover the cooker (making sure the kitchen towel is pulled taut), and cook on the low setting for 2 hours. Turn off the slow cooker and let stand, covered, for 1 hour. Do not remove the cover during the cooking or resting time.

Remove the cheesecake from the slow cooker and let cool completely on a wire rack. When cool, cover the pan tightly with plastic wrap and refrigerate until well chilled, at least 4 hours or up to overnight.

To serve, unclasp and lift off the pan sides. Using a wide metal spatula, slide the cheesecake onto a serving plate and cut into wedges. Top each serving with a scattering of blackberries (if using), and serve.

For a special presentation, top the cheesecake with Plum-Blackberry Butter (page 169) and fresh blackberries.

TRES LECHES RICE PUDDING WITH TOASTED COCONUT

Old-fashioned rice pudding gets a new look—and taste—with the addition of the flavors of Latin American *tres leches* cake. To toast the coconut, spread it on a small rimmed baking sheet and toast in a 350°F (165°C) oven, stirring a few times, until golden brown, about 5 minutes.

Unsalted butter for preparing insert

1 cup (200 g) Arborio or other short-grain white rice

1 can (14 fl oz/425 ml) coconut milk (not light), shaken well before opening

1 can (14 fl oz/425 ml) sweetened condensed milk (not light)

3½ cups (825 ml) whole milk, plus more as needed for serving

¾ cup (90 g) sweetened shredded dried coconut, toasted

1 cinnamon stick

2 teaspoons pure vanilla extract

1¼ teaspoons kosher salt

2 tablespoons firmly packed golden brown sugar (optional)

Whipped cream, for serving

Ground cinnamon, for serving

SERVES 8

Butter the insert of a slow cooker evenly.

Put the rice, coconut milk, condensed milk, 2 cups (480 ml) of the whole milk, ½ cup (60 g) of the toasted coconut, the cinnamon stick, vanilla, and salt in a slow cooker and stir to mix well. Cover and cook on the high setting for 3 hours, stirring once every hour. The rice should be tender.

Just before the rice is ready, in a small saucepan over medium heat, warm the remaining 1½ cups (350 ml) whole milk until hot. Pour the hot milk over the finished rice and stir to mix well. Turn off the slow cooker and let stand, covered, for 30 minutes.

Stir the pudding, taste, and adjust the seasoning with salt if needed. Or, if you prefer the pudding a bit sweeter, stir in the brown sugar. Transfer the pudding to a serving bowl and let cool to room temperature. Remove and discard the cinnamon stick, then cover tightly and refrigerate until cold, at least 4 hours or up to 3 days.

When ready to serve, stir a little milk into the pudding as needed to achieve the consistency you like. Spoon the pudding into individual bowls, top with whipped cream, the remaining ¼ cup (30 g) toasted coconut, and a dusting of ground cinnamon, then serve.

STICKY DATE PUDDING WITH TOFFEE SAUCE

Despite the name, this dense, deeply flavored dessert is more of a cake than a pudding. The dates add dark sweetness, while the vanilla-scented toffee sauce delivers a satisfying richness. If you like, accompany each serving with a spoonful of lightly whipped cream or a scoop of vanilla ice cream.

Unsalted butter for greasing mold, plus 4 tablespoons (60 g) unsalted butter, at cool room temperature

½ cup (70 g) pitted and finely chopped dates

¾ teaspoon baking soda

¾ cup (180 ml) boiling water, plus more for the water bath

¾ cup (155 g) firmly packed dark brown sugar

2 large eggs

2 teaspoons pure vanilla extract

1 cup (120 g) all-purpose flour

2 teaspoons baking powder

½ teaspoon kosher salt

FOR THE TOFFEE SAUCE

4 tablespoons (60 g) unsalted butter

¾ cup (155 g) firmly packed dark brown sugar

¾ cup (180 ml) heavy cream

Pinch of kosher salt

1 teaspoon pure vanilla extract

SERVES 6–8

Select an 8-cup (1.9-l) soufflé mold (about 7 inches/18 cm in diameter and 3–4 inches/7.5–10 cm deep) that will fit in your slow cooker. Lightly butter the bottom and sides of the mold, then line the bottom with a circle of parchment paper.

In a small bowl, combine the dates, baking soda, and boiling water. Let stand until cool, about 10 minutes.

In a stand mixer fitted with the paddle attachment, beat together the 4 tablespoons butter and the sugar on medium speed until fluffy and light. Add the eggs, one at a time, beating after each addition until incorporated. Beat in the vanilla. Remove the bowl from the mixer stand, add the flour, baking powder, and salt, and stir until evenly distributed. Add the date mixture and stir to mix. Scrape the batter into the prepared soufflé mold and smooth the top.

Put the soufflé mold into the slow cooker. Pour boiling water into the slow cooker to reach about halfway up the sides of the mold. Do not fill the insert more than half full. Wrap the slow cooker lid with a clean kitchen towel, cover the cooker (making sure the kitchen towel is pulled taut), and cook on the high setting for about 2 hours. The pudding is done when a toothpick inserted into the center comes out clean.

Remove the pudding from the slow cooker and set aside on a wire rack to cool for about 20 minutes. Invert the mold onto a wire rack, lift off the mold, and then gently peel off the parchment.

To make the toffee sauce, in a small, heavy saucepan over medium heat, melt the butter. Add the sugar, cream, and salt and whisk to combine. Cook, whisking constantly, until the sauce becomes sticky, about 5 minutes. Remove from the heat and stir in the vanilla.

To serve, slide the pudding onto a serving plate and top with half of the warm toffee sauce. Cut the pudding into wedges and serve the remaining sauce alongside.

Pear–Cardamom Butter (page 169) served with ginger tea cake and dusted with ground cinnamon and confectioners' sugar

Nectarine Butter (page 168) layered with plain Greek yogurt and sprinkled with chopped pistachios

Pear–Cardamom Butter (page 169) spooned atop confectioners' sugar–dusted marbelized pound cake

4 WAYS WITH FRUIT BUTTER

The slow cooker is a surprisingly good way to create fruit butters that retain the vibrant flavor of the fruit. Leaving the lid off for part of the cooking time helps condense and thicken the preserves. Use your imagination when it comes to serving.

Pumpkin Spice Butter (page 168) swirled into soft vanilla ice cream

Plum-Blackberry Butter (page 169) spooned over toasted angel food cake and topped with whipped cream and fresh mint

NECTARINE BUTTER

4 lb (1.8 kg) ripe nectarines or peaches, peeled, pitted, and finely chopped

2 cups (400 g) sugar

¼ cup (60 ml) fresh lemon juice

MAKES 5 HALF-PINT (285-ML) JARS

Put the nectarines, sugar, and lemon juice in a slow cooker and stir to mix well. Cover and cook on the low setting for 4 hours, stirring once or twice.

Uncover and use an immersion blender to purée the nectarines to the consistency you like. With the slow cooker still uncovered, cook the purée on the high setting, stirring once every 30–60 minutes, for 3½–4 hours or longer, depending on the ripeness of the fruit. The fruit butter should thicken and reduce by about half. To check the thickness, put a small saucer in the freezer. When the butter has reduced by about half, spoon a small dollop of it onto the well-chilled plate. Return the plate to the freezer for 1 minute, then push the dollop with a finger. If it mounds and holds its shape, the butter is ready. If too runny to hold its shape, continue to cook for several minutes, then test again.

Transfer the fruit butter to airtight storage containers and let cool, then cover and refrigerate for up to 3 weeks. For long-term storage, divide the butter among 5 clean half-pint (285-ml) jars with lids and process in a boiling-water bath; see page 176 for directions.

PUMPKIN SPICE BUTTER

4 lb (1.8 kg) Sugar Pie pumpkin (1 medium or 2 small)

1 cup (240 ml) apple cider or unfiltered apple juice

⅔ cup (140 g) firmly packed golden brown sugar

½ cup (155 g) maple syrup

2 teaspoons pumpkin pie spice

½ teaspoon kosher salt

MAKES 5 HALF-PINT (285-ML) JARS

Peel the pumpkin(s) with a vegetable peeler, then cut out the stem. Cut the pumpkin(s) in half. Using a spoon, scoop out and discard the seeds. Cut the flesh into 1-inch (2.5-cm) cubes; you should have about 2¾ lb (1.2 kg). Put the pumpkin cubes in a slow cooker. Add the apple cider, sugar, maple syrup, pumpkin pie spice, and salt and stir to combine. Cover and cook on the low setting for 6 hours, stirring once or twice.

Uncover and use an immersion blender to purée the pumpkin until smooth. (For a smoother butter, transfer the pumpkin and juices to a blender and process until smooth, then return the purée to the slow cooker.) To check the thickness, put a small saucer in the freezer. When the butter has reduced by about half, spoon a small dollop of it onto the well-chilled plate. Return the plate to the freezer for 1 minute, then push the dollop with a finger. If it mounds and holds its shape, the butter is ready. If too runny to hold its shape, continue to cook for several minutes, then test again.

If the butter isn't thick enough, with the slow cooker still uncovered, continue to cook on the low setting, stirring once every 30–60 minutes, for 1–2 hours.

Transfer the fruit butter to airtight storage containers and let cool, then cover and refrigerate for up to 1 month. Do not process in a boiling-water bath.

PLUM-BLACKBERRY BUTTER

2 lb (900 g) ripe plums, pitted and cut into small pieces

1½ lb (680 g) blackberries (4 pt)

2 cups (400 g) sugar

¼ cup (60 ml) fresh lemon juice

½ teaspoon five-spice powder

MAKES 5 HALF-PINT (285-ML) JARS

Put the plums, blackberries, sugar, lemon juice, and five-spice powder in a slow cooker and stir to mix well. Cover and cook on the low setting for 4 hours, stirring once or twice.

Uncover and use an immersion blender to purée the fruit to the consistency you like. With the slow cooker still uncovered, cook the purée on the high setting, stirring once every 30–60 minutes, for 6–7 hours, depending on the ripeness of the fruit. The fruit butter should thicken and reduce by about half. To check the thickness, put a small saucer in the freezer. When the butter has reduced by about half, spoon a small dollop of it onto the well-chilled plate. Return the plate to the freezer for 1 minute, then push the dollop with a finger. If it mounds and holds its shape, the butter is ready. If too runny to hold its shape, continue to cook for several minutes, then test again.

Transfer the fruit butter to airtight storage containers and let cool, then cover and refrigerate for up to 3 weeks. For long-term storage, divide the butter among 5 clean half-pint (285-ml) jars with lids and process in a boiling-water bath; see page 176 for directions.

PEAR-CARDAMOM BUTTER

4 lb (1.8 kg) Bartlett pears, halved, cored, and cut into 1-inch (2.5-cm) pieces

1 cup (200 g) granulated sugar

1 cup (210 g) firmly packed golden brown sugar

¼ cup (60 ml) fresh lemon juice

2 star anise pods

1 cinnamon stick

¼ teaspoon ground cardamom

⅛ teaspoon ground nutmeg

MAKES 5 HALF-PINT (285-ML) JARS

Put the pears, granulated and brown sugars, lemon juice, star anise, cinnamon, cardamom, and nutmeg in a slow cooker and stir to mix well. Cover and cook on the low setting for 4 hours, stirring once or twice.

Uncover and remove and discard the star anise and cinnamon stick. Use an immersion blender to purée the pears until smooth. With the slow cooker still uncovered, cook the purée on the high setting, stirring once every 30–60 minutes, for 4 hours, depending on the ripeness of the fruit. To check the thickness, put a small saucer in the freezer. When the butter has reduced by about half, spoon a small dollop of it onto the well-chilled plate. Return the plate to the freezer for 1 minute, then push the dollop with a finger. If it mounds and holds its shape, the butter is ready. If too runny to hold its shape, continue to cook for several minutes, then test again.

Transfer the fruit butter to airtight storage containers and let cool, then cover and refrigerate for up to 3 weeks. For long-term storage, divide the butter among 5 clean half-pint (285-ml) jars with lids and process in a boiling-water bath; see page 176 for directions.

STOCKS, SIDES & SAUCES

BEEF STOCK

4 lb (1.8 kg) mixed beef bones, such as neck bones, oxtails, knuckle bones, and/or bone-in short ribs

2 tablespoons olive oil

1 large carrot, peeled and coarsely chopped

1 large yellow onion, coarsely chopped

4 cloves garlic, smashed

1 tablespoon peppercorns

2 bay leaves

2 tablespoons cider vinegar

Kosher salt (optional)

MAKES ABOUT 3 QT (2.8 L)

Preheat the oven to 425°F (220°C). Spread the bones in a single layer on a large rimmed baking sheet and drizzle evenly with the oil. Roast, turning the bones once after about 30 minutes, until well browned, about 1 hour.

Transfer the roasted bones and any juices and fat from the pan to a slow cooker. Using a metal spatula, scrape up any browned bits from the pan bottom and add them as well. Add the carrot, onion, garlic, peppercorns, bay leaves, and vinegar and toss and stir to mix well. Add water to submerge the bones and vegetables completely.

Cover and cook on the low setting until the broth is dark, rich, and flavorful, 24–36 hours. During cooking, ideally about every 6 hours, check the broth and skim off any foam from the surface with a large spoon. If the level of the liquid falls below the bone mixture, add hot water as needed to cover. If the broth is not simmering rapidly, raise the heat to the high setting for the last 6 hours.

Remove and discard the large bones from the broth, then strain the broth through a fine-mesh sieve set over a large bowl or other container. Discard the solids. The broth can be seasoned to taste with salt now or just before use. Let cool to room temperature, then cover and refrigerate until the fat solidifies on the surface. Remove and discard the fat, transfer the broth to 1 or more airtight containers, and refrigerate for up to 1 week or freeze for up to 3 months.

CHICKEN STOCK

5 lb (2.3 kg) chicken backs and necks

2 carrots, coarsely chopped

1 leek, including about 6 inches (15 cm) of the green tops, cleaned and coarsely chopped

1 celery stalk, coarsely chopped

4 sprigs fresh flat-leaf parsley

2 sprigs fresh thyme, or ½ teaspoon dried thyme

¼ teaspoon peppercorns

MAKES ABOUT 2 QUARTS (1.9 L)

In a stockpot, combine the chicken, carrots, leek, celery, parsley, thyme, and peppercorns. Add cold water to cover by 1 inch (2.5 cm). Place the pot over medium-high heat and bring just to a boil, skimming off any foam that rises to the surface. Reduce the heat to low and simmer uncovered, skimming the surface as needed and adding more water if necessary to keep the ingredients immersed, until the meat has fallen off the bones and the stock is flavorful and fragrant, about 3 hours. Remove from the heat and strain the stock through a fine-mesh sieve set over a large heatproof bowl. Discard the solids in the sieve. Let the stock stand for 5 minutes, then skim off the fat from the surface. Use the stock at once or let cool to room temperature, cover, and refrigerate for up to 3 days or freeze for up to 3 months. Lift off and discard the fat congealed on the surface before using.

VEGETABLE STOCK

3 large leeks
2 yellow onions, coarsely chopped
4 carrots, coarsely chopped
3 celery stalks with leaves, chopped
¼ lb (120 g) fresh button mushrooms, brushed clean and halved
6 sprigs fresh flat-leaf parsley
2 sprigs fresh thyme, or ½ teaspoon dried thyme
¼ teaspoon peppercorns

MAKES ABOUT 2 QUARTS (1.9 L)

Trim, halve, and rinse the leeks, then cut into chunks. In a stockpot, combine the leeks, onions, carrots, celery, mushrooms, parsley, thyme, and peppercorns. Add about 2 qt (1.9 l) water to the stockpot and bring to a boil over high heat. Reduce the heat to medium-low, cover partially, and simmer until the vegetables are very soft and the flavors have blended, about 1 hour. Remove from the heat and strain the stock through a colander set over a large heatproof bowl. Press down on the solids to extract all the liquid, and discard the solids. Use the stock at once or let cool to room temperature, cover, and refrigerate for up to 3 days or freeze for up to 3 months.

FISH STOCK

2½ lb (1.1 kg) fish bones, heads, and skin, rinsed
1 large yellow onion, coarsely chopped
½ fennel bulb, trimmed and coarsely chopped
3 celery stalks, coarsely chopped
1 carrot, peeled and chopped
1 leek, including tender green parts, chopped
2 cups (475 ml) dry white wine

MAKES ABOUT 2 QUARTS (1.9 L)

In a stockpot, combine the fish, onion, fennel, celery, carrot, leek, wine, and 6 cups (1.4 l) cold water. Place the pot over medium-high heat and bring just to a boil, skimming off any foam that rises to the surface. Reduce the heat to low and simmer uncovered, skimming the surface as needed, until the stock is fragrant and flavorful, about 30 minutes. Remove from the heat and strain the stock through a colander set over a large heatproof bowl. Discard the solids in the colander. Use the stock at once or let cool to room temperature, cover, and refrigerate for up to 3 days or freeze for up to 3 months.

AIOLI

1 large egg yolk
Juice of 1 lemon (about 2 tablespoons)
1 teaspoon Dijon mustard
1 small clove garlic, minced
Kosher salt
⅔ cup (160 ml) canola oil
⅓ cup (80 ml) mild olive oil

MAKES ABOUT 1¼ CUPS (300 ML)

In a small bowl, whisk together the egg yolk, lemon juice, mustard, garlic, and a scant ½ teaspoon salt. Add the mixture to a small food processor. Turn the processor on and slowly add about half of the oil through the feed tube in a thin, slow stream. The mixture should emulsify. Now slowly pour in the remaining oil and process until incorporated. The aioli should be thick. Transfer to a bowl, cover, and refrigerate until serving or for up to 2 days.

MASHED POTATOES

3 lb (1.4 kg) russet, Yukon gold, or sweet potatoes, peeled and cut into chunks
Kosher salt and freshly ground white pepper
½ cup (4 oz/115 g) unsalted butter, at room temperature
About ½ cup (4 fl oz/120 ml) whole milk, warmed

MAKES 8–10 SERVINGS

In a large saucepan over high heat, combine the potatoes with salted water to cover and bring to a boil. Reduce the heat to medium-low and simmer until the potatoes are tender when pierced with a knife, about 20 minutes. Drain well. Return the potatoes to the pan and stir over medium-low heat for 2 minutes to evaporate the excess moisture. Press the warm potatoes through a ricer into a large bowl. (Alternatively, mash the potatoes with a potato masher.) Cut the butter into slices and scatter over the potatoes. Whisk in the butter and enough warm milk to produce the desired texture. Season to taste with salt and white pepper, then serve.

VARIATION

Herbed Mashed Potatoes

Prepare the mashed potatoes as directed. Just before serving, stir in ¼ cup (15 g) chopped flat-leaf parsley and 1 tablespoon finely chopped mixed fresh herbs, such as thyme, basil, or chives (in any combination).

CREAMY POLENTA

Kosher salt and freshly ground pepper
2 cups (340 g) coarsely ground Italian polenta (not quick cooking)
¼ cup (60 g) unsalted butter, cut into small cubes

MAKES 6 SERVINGS

In a heavy saucepan over high heat, bring 7 cups (1.75 l) water to a boil. Add 2 teaspoons salt. While stirring continuously with a whisk, gradually add the polenta until all of it has been incorporated. Switch to a wooden spoon and continue to stir constantly to prevent sticking and lumps from forming; reduce the heat until the mixture only bubbles occasionally. Cook, stirring, until the polenta is thick, smooth, and creamy, 20–25 minutes. Remove the polenta from the heat and stir in the butter, a few cubes at a time, until fully absorbed. Season to taste with salt and pepper, then serve.

VARIATION

Creamy Parmesan Polenta

Cook the polenta as directed. Just before seasoning, add ½ cup (2 oz/60 g) freshly grated Parmesan cheese and stir over low heat just until melted, then season to taste with salt and pepper.

STEAMED WHITE RICE

1½ cups (300 g) long-grain white rice, such as jasmine or basmati
2¼ cups (525 ml) water
½ teaspoon kosher salt

SERVES 6–8

In a saucepan over high heat, combine the rice, water, and salt and bring to a boil. Reduce the heat to low, give the rice a stir, then cover and cook, without lifting the lid, until the liquid is absorbed and the rice is tender, 20 minutes. Remove from the heat and let stand, covered, for 10 minutes. Uncover, fluff with a fork, and serve.

VARIATION

Cilantro-Lime Rice

Cook the rice as directed. Just before serving, stir in ½ cup (30 g) loosely packed chopped fresh cilantro and the juice of 1 lime, or more as needed.

STEAMED BROWN RICE

1½ cups (300 g) short-grain brown rice
3 cups (700 ml) water
½ teaspoon kosher salt

SERVES 6–8

In a saucepan over high heat, combine the rice, water, and salt and bring to a boil. Reduce the heat to low, give the rice a stir, then cover and cook, without lifting the lid, until the liquid is absorbed and the rice is tender, 45–50 minutes. Remove from the heat and let stand, covered, for 10 minutes. Uncover, fluff with a fork, and serve.

ROASTED ROOT VEGETABLES

3 tablespoons canola oil

2 lb (900 g) root vegetables such as Yukon gold or other thin-skinned potatoes, sweet potatoes or yams, parsnips, carrots, and/or rutabagas

Kosher salt and freshly ground pepper

1 tablespoon chopped fresh flat-leaf parsley (optional)

MAKES 6–8 SERVINGS

Preheat the oven to 425°F (220°C). Drizzle half the oil onto each of 2 rimmed baking sheets. Place the sheets in the oven to preheat while you prepare the vegetables. Peel the root vegetables, then cut the potatoes or rutabagas into 1½-inch chunks or the parsnips and carrots into pieces about ½ inch (12 mm) thick and 2–3 inches (5- to 7.5-cm) long. Remove the baking sheets from the oven and divide the vegetables between them. Toss the vegetables to coat them with the oil, sprinkle lightly with salt and pepper, and arrange in a single layer. Roast, stirring once or twice, until browned and tender, 30–45 minutes. Sprinkle with parsley (if using) and serve.

ZUCCHINI NOODLES

6 medium-size zucchini

1 teaspoon kosher salt

2 tablespoons olive oil

SERVES 6

Using a spiralizer, spiralize the zucchini using the shredder blade. Toss with the salt and place in a colander; let the liquid drain from the zucchini for 30 minutes. In a large frying' pan over medium-high heat, warm the oil. When oil is hot, add the zucchini and sauté, stirring often, just until warmed through, about 30 seconds; do not overcook.

SAUTÉED GREENS

¼ cup (60 ml) extra-virgin olive oil

1 large bunch curly kale or Swiss chard, stems removed and leaves coarsely chopped

2 garlic cloves, thinly sliced

1 small red chile, stemmed and thinly sliced (optional)

Kosher salt and freshly ground pepper

SERVES 4

In a large frying pan over medium-high heat, warm the oil. Add the kale, garlic, and chile (if using) and sauté until the kale is wilted and the garlic is lightly golden, 2–4 minutes. Season with salt and pepper, then serve.

VEGETABLE SLAW

1 cup (90 g) coarsely shredded green cabbage

1 cup (90 g) coarsely shredded red cabbage

½ cup (45 g) shredded carrot

1 small red bell pepper, seeded and cut into matchsticks

¼–½ teaspoon sugar

Kosher salt and freshly ground pepper

3 tablespoons extra-virgin olive oil

2 tablespoons cider vinegar

MAKES ABOUT 4 CUPS (360 G)

In a bowl, combine the green cabbage, red cabbage, carrot, bell pepper, sugar to taste, ½ teaspoon salt and a few grinds of pepper and toss to mix. Drizzle with the oil and vinegar and toss to mix.

PICKLED ONIONS

1 large red onion, halved and sliced

6 tablespoons (90 ml) rice vinegar

1 garlic clove, minced

¼ teaspoon dried oregano

1 teaspoon sugar

½ teaspoon kosher salt

MAKES ABOUT 2 CUPS (180 G)

Place the onions in a heatproof bowl and add boiling water to cover. Let soak for 2–3 minutes. Drain well. In a saucepan over medium-high heat, bring the vinegar, garlic, oregano, sugar, and salt to a boil, whisking until the sugar dissolves. Add the onion, stir, and remove from the heat. Set aside to cool to room temperature. Let stand for 1 hour before using, or transfer to an airtight container and refrigerate for up to 2 weeks.

MANGO SALSA

2 mangoes, peeled, pitted, and diced (about 2 cups/310 g)
½ small red bell pepper, seeded and finely diced
1 small serrano chile, seeded and minced
4 green onions, including tender green parts, thinly sliced
¼ cup (15 g) coarsely chopped fresh cilantro
1½ tablespoons fresh lime juice
¼–½ teaspoon kosher salt

MAKES ABOUT 3 CUPS (460 G)

In a bowl, combine the mangoes, bell pepper, chile, green onions, cilantro, lime juice, and salt to taste. Toss together gently, cover, and refrigerate for at least 30 minutes or up to 1 hour before serving.

CORN SALSA

1 teaspoon Dijon mustard
1 tablespoon white wine vinegar
1 teaspoon finely grated lime zest
2 tablespoons fresh lime juice
Kosher salt and freshly ground pepper
¼ cup (60 ml) extra-virgin olive oil
2 cups (340 g) fresh or thawed, frozen corn kernels
2 cups (340 g) grape or cherry tomatoes, halved
4 green onions, including tender green tops, thinly sliced

MAKES ABOUT 4½ CUPS (810 G)

In a small bowl, whisk together the mustard, vinegar, lime zest and juice, ½ teaspoon salt, and a few grinds of pepper, then whisk in the oil to make a vinaigrette. In a bowl, combine the corn, tomatoes, green onions, and enough vinaigrette to coat lightly. Toss well to mix, adding more vinaigrette as needed.

TANGY DIPPING SAUCE

⅔ cup (175 ml) water
2 tablespoons sugar
2 tablespoons rice vinegar
¼ cup (60 ml) fish sauce
¼ cup (60 ml) fresh lime juice
1 small fresh red Thai chile, seeded and finely chopped
1 small clove garlic, minced

MAKES ABOUT 1 CUP (240 ML)

In a small saucepan over medium heat, combine the water, sugar, and vinegar and bring to a boil, stirring until the sugar dissolves. Remove from the heat and stir in the fish sauce, lime juice, chile, and garlic. Let cool to room temperature before serving. Store in an airtight container in the refrigerator for up to 3 days.

LIME-SOY VINAIGRETTE

1 tablespoon extra-virgin olive oil
1½ tsp reduced-sodium soy sauce
Juice of ½ lime
½ teaspoon peeled and minced fresh ginger
Pinch of sugar
1 or 2 drops hot pepper sauce such as Tabasco
Pinch of salt

MAKES ABOUT ½ CUP (120 ML)

In a blender or mini food processor, combine the oil, soy sauce, lime juice, ginger, sugar, hot pepper sauce to taste, and ⅛ teaspoon salt and process for 15 seconds to emulsify.

CHEDDAR BISCUITS

2 cups (240 g) all-purpose flour
2 teaspoons baking powder
½ teaspoon baking soda
¾ teaspoon kosher salt
1¼ cups (300 ml) buttermilk
½ cup (120 g) unsalted butter, melted and cooled slightly
½ cup (60 g) shredded Cheddar cheese

MAKES 12 BISCUITS

Position a rack in the upper third of the oven and preheat the oven to 400°F (200°C). Line a large rimmed baking sheet with parchment paper.

In a bowl, using a fork, stir together the flour, baking powder, baking soda, and salt. Add the buttermilk, melted butter, and cheese and stir gently just until the flour is moistened and the ingredients are thoroughly blended.

Drop 12 equal-size blobs of the batter onto the prepared baking sheet, spacing them at least 1–2 inches (2.5–5-cm) apart. Bake until golden and puffed, 15–18 minutes.

CROSTINI

1 baguette, cut on the diagonal into slices ⅜ inch (1 cm) thick (about 24 slices)
2 tablespoons olive oil
2 cloves garlic, peeled but left whole

MAKES 24 CROSTINI; SERVES 8–12

Preheat the oven to 425°F (220°C). Brush the baguette slices on both sides with the oil and arrange in a single layer on a rimmed baking sheet. Toast, turning once, until nicely browned on both sides, about 7 minutes. While the toasts are still warm, rub one side of each toast with the garlic.

TECHNIQUE
Fruit Butter Preserving

To keep the fruit butter shelf stable at room temperature for up to 1 year, follow these steps for boiling water processing. Have ready 5 clean half-pint (285-ml) jars with self-sealing lids and metal screw bands. Select a pot that will hold all of the jars in a single layer and add water to a depth of about 2 inches (5 cm). Bring the water to a simmer over medium heat. Reduce the heat to low and place the empty jars in the pan, laying them side down. Add the lids and bands and simmer for 10 minutes.

Lay a kitchen towel on a work surface. Remove the jars from the pot and set them upside down to drain on the kitchen towel. Retrieve the lids and bands and set them alongside the jars on the towel. While the jars are still hot, fill them with the hot fruit butter, dividing it evenly and leaving at least ½-inch (12-mm) headspace. Using a damp kitchen towel, wipe the rims clean, then cover each jar with a flat lid and gently secure the lid with a metal band.

Put a small rack or a folded kitchen towel in the bottom of the pot of water used for sterilizing the jars and return the water to a boil. Using a jar lifter or tongs, carefully lower the jars into the boiling water so they are standing upright with a little space between them. When the water returns to a boil, reduce the heat slightly to maintain a gentle boil, cover the pot, and boil for 10 minutes.

Using the jar lifter or tongs, transfer the jars to the towel-covered work surface, placing them upright, and let cool completely. To check if the seal on each jar is good, press down on the center of the lid with a fingertip. If the lid remains concave, rather than pops up, the seal is good. Store the jars in a cool, dark place for up to 1 year. Store any jars that fail to seal in the refrigerator for up to 3 weeks.

INDEX

EVERYDAY SLOW COOKING

Conceived and produced by Weldon Owen, Inc.
In collaboration with Williams Sonoma, Inc.
3250 Van Ness Avenue, San Francisco, CA 94109

A WELDON OWEN PRODUCTION

1150 Brickyard Cove Road
Richmond, CA 94801
www.weldonowen.com

Copyright © 2018 Weldon Owen International
and Williams Sonoma, Inc.
All rights reserved, including the right of
reproduction in whole or in part in any form.

Printed in China

10 9 8 7 6 5 4 3 2 1
2024 2023 2022 2021 2020

Library of Congress Cataloging-in-Publication
data is available.

ISBN: 978-1-68188-661-9

WELDON OWEN INTERNATIONAL

President & Publisher Roger Shaw
SVP, Sales & Marketing Amy Kaneko
Finance & Operations Director Thomas Morgan

Associate Publisher Amy Marr
Senior Editor Lisa Atwood

Creative Director Kelly Booth
Art Director Marisa Kwek
Production Designer Howie Severson

Production Director Michelle Duggan
Production Manager Sam Bissell
Imaging Manager Don Hill

Photographer John Kernick
Food Stylist Lillian Kang
Prop Stylist Kerrie Sherrell Walsh

ACKNOWLEDGMENTS

Weldon Owen wishes to thank the following people for their generous support
in producing this book: Rizwan A. Alvi, Lesley Bruynesteyn, Josephine Hsu, Heidi Ladendorf,
Veronica Laramie, Eve Lynch, Alexis Mersel, Elizabeth Parson, and Sharon Silva.